Bo

FAYE ALDRIDGE

MW00827005

MORE STORIES OF MIRACLES AND DIVINE INTERVENTION
UNDENIABLE PROOF OF LIFE AFTER DEATH

Real
Messages *from*
Heaven

Presenting
Evidence of His Presence

Davis Jackson Publishers, 332 Midtown Trail, Mt. Juliet, TN 37122
Telephone (615) 973-6908.

Printed in the U.S.A.

Editor: Peggy Culbert, Sewell, New Jersey, 08080

Interior layout and cover by Alison Griffin, www.amGriffinDesign.com
Author Photo: Jacob Layne

Etch A Sketch is a registered trademark of Ohio Art.

For inquiries about story submissions or interviews pertaining to future books, please call (615) 973-6908. Thank you!

Acknowledgments

I offer my sincere thanks to all of the dear people who allowed me to share their incredible stories in the following pages. Telling each story is a way of offering praise and honor to God for allowing us to see His blessed hope in every phase and circumstance of our lives. I say to each person who shared a story and befriended me during this endeavor, thank you, from the bottom of my heart!

Please know that you are a part of something wonderful! You are a part of this undertaking because each and every story helped make this book into a vessel carrying God's treasures to others who will be blessed by your kindness! I appreciate you for allowing others to grow their faith by understanding how God worked in your lives! God sent each of you a gift and you were good stewards willing to share your gifts with others! May you be blessed always!

Thank you Readers! As you read this book you will discover evidence of God's extraordinary presence in the lives of ordinary people. I hope that causes you to search for evidence of His presence in your own lives! Included in this book are stories like those in *Real Messages from Heaven*, Volumes 1 and 2 and more! You will discover 50 stories about these topics.

- After-Death-Appearances
- Angel Appearances
- Answers to Prayer
- Conversion Experiences
- Signs & Wonders
- Glimpses of Heaven & Hell
- Everyday Miracles

Some of these touching stories remind us that death is the end here and the beginning there, in Heaven or hell. These Supernatural Occurrences offer us the occasions to pause and examine our lives! Through these life changing experiences that you are about to read, God is speaking to us even now! Remember, we are not without hope! Jesus Christ is our hope and He is drawing our attention to Himself through these Miraculous Occurrences! May we not take them lightly.

> *Therefore, since we are receiving a kingdom that cannot be shaken, let us be thankful, and so worship God acceptably with reverence and awe* (Hebrews 12:28 NIV).

Thank you Peggy Culbert for your integrity, assistance, participation and expertise as the Editor!

Thank you Alison Griffin for your proficiencies in the interior and exterior design of this book!

Thank you Timothy Burrow, Attorney/Author for making available all of your resources as needed!

Thank you Phyllis Carman for your prayerful support during this endeavor and in the days ahead!

Thank you Jacob Layne for your time and photography skills!

Dedication

To The Most High God,
the God of Abraham, Isaac and Jacob,
because each chapter in this book represents
a gift that You gave to someone!

Without You, there would be no book!
Therefore, this book is humbly and lovingly
dedicated to You, Lord!

Thank You!

Table of Contents

Chapter 1

Honey, Don't Cry

Truly, truly, I say to you, he who believes has eternal life (John 6:47).

Valerie Vorpahl grew up with her parents in rural Wisconsin in the late seventies and early eighties. Her family lived near her mom's parents and that made Valerie entirely happy! In the summer time, she hurried to finish her chores at home whether it was cutting the grass, working in the barn, the garden or the kitchen so she could go to her grandparents' nearby farm. Her uncle and aunt lived on the farm also and Valerie enjoyed keeping their little ones while they did farm work. There was always something in need of repair and every hand was a welcome hand when it came to keeping the place up.

Working with her Grandpa was Valerie's favorite thing to do! He was an unusual person and a wonderful grandfather! His name was Peter Dogs. Peter was a large man, standing 6 feet 6 inches tall, weighing a little over 300 pounds. He was strong and tough; however, his heart was a gentle one and Valerie owned a portion of it.

Having been adopted into the family, Valerie was naturally different in some ways from those who were blood relatives. Valerie tried hard to fit in perfectly, but her heart was unique and so was her point of view. As a young girl, her Grandpa taught her not to feel uncomfortable about that reality; instead he insisted that she embrace her differences. Both grandparents made her feel just right by accepting her in all her honesty. They surrounded her with love and taught her by example the ways of faith.

Valerie's Grandpa and Grandma loved the Lord and their lives reflected their devotion to God. They worshiped in the same little Lutheran Church all their lives and Valerie accompanied them on many occasions. Learning about God and Biblical matters intrigued her from an early age. She was eager to learn about Jesus and faith. Valerie and her parents attended a United Church of Christ. Both families were grounded in their belief in God and Heaven and those convictions helped shape young Valerie into a Christian early in her life.

By the time Valerie turned 24 years old she had married and given birth to two adorable little boys! Her husband was a truck driver for a company that hired him to drive long distances for prolonged periods of time. Valerie had opened her own hair salon and rarely had a few minutes to stop and rest. Her Grandpa made it his business to call her every night, just checking to make sure that she and the boys were alright.

One particular night that Peter called Valerie was different. He engaged her in an unusually long conversation. Valerie was so tired that all she wanted to do was fall into bed and go soundly to sleep. The children were asleep, finally, and she tried to cut the conversation short, but without success. For some strange reason, Peter just could not bring himself to say "good night" to Valerie. He seemed to be concerned for her and the boys, expressing his desire for them to be safe, well, and cared for by a strong and loving husband and father. He needed to know she was going to be alright, no matter what. After a while, the conversation ended and Valerie eagerly crawled into bed.

Only fifteen minutes later, Valerie received a phone call from her Grandmother, saying Grandpa had just experienced a heart attack. He died just minutes after he reached the hospital by ambulance.

Standing next to her husband's still body, through tears, his wife remarked, "He is in God's hands now." She had reason to be certain about that, for he was truly a man saved by God's grace. He lived his faith. That was a comforting thought, for death came that night without warning, as it often does in this fragile earthly life.

In the days following the death, Valerie cried and cried! She had never shed so many tears in her entire lifetime. She was sad for those loved ones who would miss her grandfather, but mainly she was sad because she could not imagine her own life without him. As a young Christian experiencing the death of a loved one, those days became a difficult trial of her faith. Valerie felt an unbearable grief and a longing desire to have her grandfather alive and well the way he was before death came so suddenly.

Three days after Peter died something life changing happened that would affect Valerie for the rest of her life! Her husband was sound asleep in bed, lying next to her. Valerie was sitting up in bed, reclining, about to lie down next to her husband in search of sleep. There in the stillness she sat with tears in her eyes, engrossed in her thoughts about the past three days.

Valerie was staring straight ahead into the partially darkened room when suddenly, her deceased Grandfather materialized right before her eyes! She blinked her eyes hard several times, thinking he would disappear but that did not happen! Valerie was startled by the apparition standing in her bedroom! She thought she was seeing things and she was! She was seeing her deceased grandfather actually standing at the foot of her bed! The deceased man was wearing his favorite striped bib overalls and red plaid shirt! On his head, there rested his favorite barnyard hat. It was a white baseball cap with red polka dots!

Standing there with a faint light glowing around his body, in his usual voice, Peter kindly spoke directly to his granddaughter. He used the same affectionate pet name he always called her saying, "Honey, don't cry for me! I'm okay, I'm with my Father. Please don't cry!" Valerie was wide eyed and nearly in disbelief! At the same time, she was overjoyed and hesitant about taking her eyes off him!

Valerie turned quickly to awaken her sleeping husband, wanting him to experience the After-Death-Appearance, the supernatural occurrence that was in progress! She glanced back toward the foot of the bed where Peter was just standing! He had vanished without another word!

That After-Death-Appearance was a powerful thing! It deepened Valerie's faith in ways in which she could never have imagined. All the Bible truths she had ever learned from her parents and grandparents years ago became incredibly real to her after that miraculous visitation! She had just witnessed an experience that was genuine proof of life after death! Her thoughts were racing! She wanted to laugh and cry simultaneously!

The After-Death-Appearance was a gift to Valerie and now it is a gift to others who have lost loved ones and are in need of affirmation that what the Bible teaches us is real and true. There are two worlds; the one we can see and the one we cannot see! Accepting Jesus comes with great rewards; one of which is the promise of eternal life for the ones who have received Salvation through Christ Jesus our Lord! Death comes without warning! Valerie would ask each reader one question if she could today. Out of deep concern she would ask each one of us, "Are you prepared to die if today is your last day?"

Jesus answered, "I am the way and the truth and the life. No one comes to the Father except through Me" (John 14:6 NIV).

Chapter 2

Not in the Box

For God so loved the world, that He gave His only begotten Son, that whoever believes in Him should not perish, but have eternal life (John 3:16).

Timmy Brough[1] was only nine years old when his grandfather passed away. Timmy's much loved Poppa, died suddenly one rainy Friday afternoon in June. That was his first experience with death and it caused him to feel frightened, sad, and angry at the same time. Timmy's dad tried to explain matters to him in ways he could grasp; however, nothing made sense to the child on that life changing day.

The celebration of life for the deceased took place on a Sunday afternoon at a funeral home not far from where the family lived. The funeral was scheduled for the next day. The much loved grandfather had lived in the same small rural community all of his life and almost everyone in the county knew him. On the day of visitation at the funeral home, there was standing room only inside the building. Many people gathered outside in front of the building, reminiscing about the life and death of the deceased. He was well thought of and the outpouring of sympathetic guests was indicative of that fact. He had believed strongly in God and had lived his life accordingly.

Timmy's dad held his hand as they approached the casket in which his grandfather's body had been placed. The small child anxiously looked all around the room. The people looked like trees. Because of his small stature, his eyes mainly saw waistbands and

---

1

mid sections of people, not their faces. In his young mind he did not see the throngs of people as humans. All that was happening seemed very bizarre! When the child looked into the face of his deceased grandfather, he saw what appeared to be a mannequin who looked like his Poppa. Timmy felt like he was trapped in a very bad dream!

Timmy wished he could stop smelling the flowers in the floral arrangements that were placed all around the room. The strong sweet fragrance was overpowering and sickeningly sweet. At that time he associated the sweet fragrance with death, sadness, and saying goodbye to one whom he loved dearly. Waves of despair swept over Timmy each time he made his way through the crowd of people and flowers the rest of the afternoon.

The little boy refused to cry until that day. When he could restrain his tears no longer Timmy allowed them to roll down his face. Sadness in the form of tears trickled from the corners of his eyes. He ran toward a rear side door searching for a way of escaping!

Timmy was biting his lip and hoping no one would follow him! He was pleased when he saw he was finally alone. One more whiff of roses, chrysanthemums or lilies would have been too much. He walked slowly onto the sprawling green lawn toward a large lone oak tree. Keeping his back turned toward the building Timmy finished his cry in private. He leaned against the tree trunk staring into the distance, wishing his Poppa would get out of that box and come outside to find him. He would make everything alright; Timmy just knew he would! How he longed to feel those familiar strong and loving arms hugging him once again!

The touch of a hand on his small shoulder surprised Timmy, but not nearly as much as the recognizable voice did! He turned quickly and discovered his Poppa was standing there smiling, staring down at him! He looked the same as he did last week when they went fishing at the creek! He was wearing a casual white shirt and black slacks like he usually wore on Sundays. Suits were not his favorite clothes! Timmy wanted to yell, throw his arms around him, and hug him tightly, but he was unable to move or speak! His body appeared to be frozen strangely. Thankfully, his eyes and ears were working perfectly!

In his ordinary deep voice, Poppa kindly explained his departure to Timmy. He said the Lord had called him home, to go to Heaven ahead of Timmy and his family. Poppa described his new home, the place in which he would be living as absolutely perfect! He said the grass was greener there and the rivers there were crystal clear! Flowers grew nearly everywhere in that special place! After all, it was Heaven! It sounded just like Poppa's farm only even more beautiful!

The old gentleman told his grandson that in Heaven no one gets sick or dies. "There," he added, "no one ever leaves their loved ones behind and no one ever says goodbye!" He assured the boy that he would see him again when it was his turn to leave the earth. Suddenly, Timmy could move normally and he lifted his right arm and wiped both teary eyes on his sleeve. When he looked up again he saw no one. Timmy's grandfather had disappeared!

Timmy smiled. The ache was gone from his chest and the emotional weight that was on his shoulders moments ago had vanished! He ran to the door and once inside, he made his way through the crowd, finding his way to the casket. When he looked at the body of his grandfather, it was with a new comprehension. He clearly understood that what he was looking at was merely the shell in which his Poppa once lived. The real live Poppa was not in the box! He was out there somewhere beyond the blue clear sky, enjoying his new life and living in a wonderful place! Timmy comprehended that he would join his grandfather in Heaven one day. The After-Death-Appearance changed Timmy's life!

Later that same day, Timmy told his parents about the visit, but they seemed skeptical. Their unbelief did not diminish his joy or hinder Timmy's certainty of what he saw, heard, and felt that day! Their reaction led the boy to keep his experience to himself for many years. In later years Timmy shared the story with others who had experienced similar occurrences and realized After-Death-Appearances are quite common. They are very natural-supernatural manifestations! God was there to help Timmy on his worst day and He will do the same for us. God provides us with peace and comfort when we need it the most if only we will believe!

If you believe, you will receive whatever you ask for in prayer (Matthew 21:22 NIV).

Chapter 3

Globe of Light

Peace I leave with you; My peace I give to you; not as the world gives do I give to you. Do not let your heart be troubled, nor let it be fearful (John 14:27).

Gary Smith[2] grew up during the eighties in one of the older established neighborhoods on the outskirts of Memphis, Tennessee. He graduated from college in 1992. Gary was unable to find a job in Memphis and he decided to move to St. Louis, Missouri where he accepted a temporary position. He needed the money and reasoned that he would be exposed to an alternative work and learning experience so the move would not be unprofitable. The parents of a college friend offered him an attic space apartment above their home, free of charge, so he jumped at the prospect. Gary was young and eager to get on with his life and he saw the open door as an exciting adventure!

Nearly four months into his new undertaking led Gary to a Friday night that seemed ordinary at first. He met a friend at a restaurant where they had dinner; then he returned to his attic space living quarters around nine p.m. He raised his window, hoping to catch a stirring breeze. It was late September and the cool night air was refreshing. Gary left all the lights out except for the one in the bathroom and that created a shadowy effect in the rest of his space. There in the partial darkness he could go unnoticed propping his body up in the extended box window seat enjoying the night air.

2

Less than five minutes passed when out of nowhere, a shimmering globe of white light zoomed through the window! It was the size of a softball! It spun around and around, looping the entire circumference of the room before it leveled out and soared past Gary's face as it flew out of the room disappearing into the night sky!

Gary was positively stunned and nearly in disbelief! He was understandably shaken and even more so when the name of his best friend, Todd, entered his mind like a message written on an aerial advertising banner being pulled by a propeller-driven airplane! No words were spoken. The knowledge came telepathically and promptly as the white ball of light zoomed out of the room! It all happened so fast leaving no actual proof behind except for an eerie feeling and a very vivid memory impressed upon Gary's mind!

Sleep did not come easily that night and Gary arose early the next morning. By seven o'clock Gary was on the phone with his mom in Memphis for their weekly chat. Nearly the first words out of his mom's mouth rendered him speechless. She said, "Gary, I have some terrible news. Your friend Todd was leaving Jackson last night on his way home to Memphis when a car veered into his lane causing a head on collision. Todd was killed instantly."

Gary shared with his mom what he had experienced the night before and they were both baffled, since neither one of them had ever had an experience like that before. Still, Gary knew in his heart the occurrence was very significant or it would not have happened. Clearly he understood that Todd's spirit had visited him in an After-Death-Appearance and the whole thing made him feel exuberant, enthusiastic and wonderful! Proof! Absolute proof was what he had experienced! Proof of life after death! If he had ever doubted the existence of God and a hereafter, he would never ever be so foolish as to doubt God again!

Gary shared the experience with Todd's grieving parents and they received the news as genuine and authentic! Years later they admitted that hearing of Todd's After-Death-Appearance had helped them get through the worst days before the passage of time took them to a place of peace and acceptance. Through it all, their faith sustained them. They were able to cling to hope more assuredly because of what Gary experienced!

May the God of hope fill you with all joy and peace as you trust in Him, so that you may overflow with hope by the power of the Holy Spirit (Romans 15:13 NIV).

Chapter 4

A Glimpse of Hell

Fear not them which kill the body, but are not able to kill the soul: but rather fear Him which is able to destroy both soul and body in hell (Matthew 10:28).

Jim McKnight was a typical Southern California boy who became a teenager in the early 1960's. He spent a lot of time at the beach with his friends and making music in his own little rock band. Jim's favorite cousin, Jesse, lived in Orosi, California, near Fresno. When Jim turned 13 he was old enough to catch a bus bound for Orosi on numerous occasions, going for long weekends at his uncle's home. Hanging out there with Jesse was Jim's favorite thing to do. Jesse's dad grew cotton on a ranch and those sprawling acres presented two inquisitive teens with endless opportunities, ample space to spread their wings, and numerous places to explore!

Jim and Jesse experimented with the tractor, popping wheelies and seeing how fast it would go until they saw Uncle Jesse, Sr. coming their way. The boys could judge his disposition by watching to see how fast he was walking. If he was walking at a fast clip, they were quick to settle down! Jesse's dad was a good man. They imagined his scolding to be worse than a beating even though he never struck them. He was a no nonsense guy and he expected the boys to do some form of physical labor on the farm for a part of each day.

On other days, Jim and Jesse rose early and walked in the orange grove, picking the largest oranges and promptly devouring them.

They spent hours talking about unimportant things, day dreaming, and enjoying the warm sunshine. Those simple bygone days Jim spent with Jesse were happy times. Those long gone summers are near and dear to Jim's heart to this very day.

The years passed quickly and Jim's life changed significantly in a short period of time. He was influenced greatly by some of the people he met and relationships that followed. Sadly, he began to experiment with drugs because some of his acquaintances had taken that route. Unfortunately, it seemed to be expected and acceptable by many of his peers.

In 1968, Jim and Pam, his new bride of three months, were living with his parents in Carson, California. Jim and Pam were very young, each one searching for something just out of reach. Sadly, Jim's life was dominated by his obsessive need to get high on drugs. He could not understand the power that controlled his thoughts and desires every waking moment, pushing him to get his hands on more and more drugs. He was within the devil's reach and out of control.

Jim's mom was a strong Christian woman belonging to a Baptist Church. She had prayed for Jim's deliverance and conversion for years and she had no intention of giving up on him. She made sure that Jim went to church when he was younger, but Jim went grudgingly and the minute the doors opened after service, he was quick to make a run for it! He wanted no part of God! However, even in those days of Jim's strong resistance to God, he was able to recognize God's efforts to draw him to Himself, but each time he rejected God's invitation to change.

A day of reckoning arrived. It was late one Saturday afternoon when Jim, at the age of 18, became the victim of Satan's fury that can only be described as an assassination attempt by way of a drug overdose. The evil demon that controlled Jim's desire for more drugs and longer highs was crying out for fulfillment. Jim responded by giving in to taking more drugs until the excessive amount became deadly. Satan desires to steal, kill and destroy and his desire was to annihilate Jim McKnight that day.

> *The thief comes only to steal and kill and destroy; I (Jesus Christ) came that they may have life, and have it abundantly* (John 10:10).

Jim collapsed on the kitchen floor as a result of the drug overdose. His life passed before his eyes, one frame at a time and what he saw was not a pretty picture. Jim saw himself rejecting Jesus over and over again and he felt so ashamed! Next Jim experienced his body in a free fall, spiraling backwards into a bottomless canyon. He saw the things of earth hurling past him as he spiraled deeper and deeper into the blackness at an increasingly rapid rate of descent! He no longer had control of his body!

Indescribable fear engulfed Jim, threatening to take his breath away! There are no words to describe the terror that gripped the lost man's mind and emotions. He felt an internal emptiness and a foreboding sense of hopelessness and helplessness!

Abruptly, Jim stopped in midair! He was paralyzed and unable to move even one finger! Panic set in! He realized he was hanging in midair, suspended by a narrow thread beneath his body. Then some words appeared before him as Jesus spoke saying, "You rejected Me, now look…" The powerless, dying and hell-bound man clearly saw a replay of each and every time that Jesus had convicted his heart! He saw the Holy Spirit urging him to surrender his life to God, and each time he had rejected Him. Jim was filled with remorse and regret inexpressible. How he wished he could go back and live his life differently! Jim knew he was condemned; he was dangling over hell, over his eternal prison of darkness where his rebellion toward God had taken him to his eternal home in hell! The terror that surged through him was unrelenting. Hell was far more wretched than he had ever imagined!

Jim could hear himself screaming in terror within the confines of his own mind! At the same time, somewhere out there he could hear the soft voice of his praying mother crying out to God on his behalf, unceasingly praying for God to "Have mercy on him and save him"!

Finally, Jim found the inner strength to call out saying, "God, if I haven't pushed You too far, I ask Your forgiveness! Please save me!" Jim spoke those words repeatedly. At first, the hopelessness prevailed, then ever so slowly, he felt his body ascending upward until he saw a faint shimmer of light! It was like he was trying to surface from the depths of the ocean. After what seemed like an eternity, Jim felt himself entering his lifeless body! His mom and Pam were kneeling beside his body on the floor praying over him as he came back to life, as his spirit re-entered his earthly shell!

Jim willingly and openly received Jesus Christ as his Savior that night and Pam accepted Jesus as her Savior at that time also! It was a night filled with God's love, mercy, grace, and forgiveness; a time of grateful rejoicing! God had given Jim a second chance! It was a time of miracles!

A few months later, Jim and his family moved to Oklahoma where he was earning a living as a painter. In 1971 he was attending a home worship service one evening, at which time he received the Baptism of the Holy Spirit! A short time later, Jim enthusiastically entered

Rhema Bible School where he studied to become a pastor. When he left Rhema, Jim began serving God as an Evangelist throughout the United States and Canada. Presently Jim's life remains totally immersed in God's business of leading others to Christ!

Today Jim leaves each one of us with an important reminder. "If you are praying for a loved one, someone who is lost, don't stop praying! Stick with it until God answers your prayers. A praying mom who refused to give up is why Jesus gave me one more chance. Mom's prayers kept me out of hell for eternity! If you love a person, you must not give up praying for their eternal Salvation! Never, ever give up!"

Be joyful in hope, patient in affliction, faithful in prayer (Romans 12:12 NIV).

Pray without ceasing (1 Thessalonians 5:17).

Chapter 5

In His Wallet

My soul, wait in silence for God only, for my hope is from Him (Psalm 62:5).

Joanie Fowinkle's parents lived in Wiggins, Mississippi when their house caught fire from a faulty lamp in the master bedroom. Joanie's mom suffered third degree burns on the entire right side of her body from head to toe. She survived only because her husband, Jay, dragged her out of the bedroom through the flames and to safety that night. The rest of the home was miraculously saved from the fire.

After hearing about the tragedy, Joanie left her home in Tallahassee, Florida and rushed to her mother's bedside at a hospital in Gulfport, Mississippi. The burn victim was suffering terribly and came close to death twice at which times the medical staff resuscitated her. In addition to the burns, she was already suffering from terminal cancer.

For a full week Joanie stayed in Mississippi with her mom at the hospital in the day time and she stayed with her dad every night. In spite of the circumstances, Joanie and Jay shared deeply meaningful time together during that week. Each of them expressed their innermost feelings, sharing many stories and personal memories that were important, but had never been spoken of before. Amazingly, often after a tragedy, the life priorities of those involved change significantly. What is most important finds its way to the surface during divinely orchestrated visits and conversations.

Jay told Joanie that in the months leading up to the fire, he had actually felt closer to God than at any other period in his lifetime. Those words were valuable at that particular time to Joanie, but would become even more valuable in the days ahead. Joanie stayed with her mom for a full week, then returned to Tallahassee to her work. She was a teacher at a school, and final exams were approaching. She felt assured that was the right thing to do.

Then, only days after Joanie returned home she received the terrible news. At first, she thought the call was to inform her of her mother's death, but she was mistaken. She was very surprised to learn that her dad had suffered a heart attack for which he was transported to Keesler Medical Center in Biloxi, Mississippi. He died just hours after he arrived at the Medical Center. His death occurred five days before he and his wife would have celebrated their 46th wedding anniversary.

Later that evening, Joanie's husband, Charley, was out walking on the beach and shedding tears over losing his father-in-law whom he loved like his own father. Meanwhile, Joanie was in their bathroom packing toiletries, preparing for the trip to Mississippi for her dad's funeral when something most unusual happened!

Joanie was working in total silence, thinking about everything that had transpired over the last few days when she heard her father's distinct voice speaking to her! He said, "Sweetheart, when you get to Keesler, ask for my belongings and in my wallet there is $107.00. Give it to Cathy; she needs it."

The man had been dead for 10 hours when he spoke those words to Joanie. Joanie could not explain how that supernatural communication happened, but she was very much aware that God had either allowed it or He had caused it. Cathy was Joanie's sister, a single-mom raising two small children and living on a small salary.

Very early the next morning, Joanie and Charley drove to Pensacola to pick up Cathy on the way to the funeral. They shared the After-Death message with Cathy and of course she cried when she heard of her dad's concern for her even after his own death! When they arrived at Keesler Medical Center, Joanie asked for her dad's personal effects. In his wallet there was exactly $107.00.

The funeral was difficult with Joanie's mom still in critical condition, but through it all, her dad's After-Death message was very comforting to the entire family! The evening after the funeral, Charley cooked a spaghetti dinner for the family at Joanie's parents' home. Charley was an excellent cook and cooking made him feel useful and temporarily eased the grief for at least a little while. After dinner He went into the guest bathroom; he had just closed the door and was standing there, when he experienced a brief visit from his deceased father-in-law, Jay!

Very clearly and very loudly, Jay spoke saying, "Thank you Charley for taking care of my family!" It startled Charley so much that he fell against the louvered closet doors behind him, almost falling to the floor! It was a second time God had allowed Jay to speak from beyond the grave and this earthly life!

It is truly amazing how our perception of death changes when we are able to accurately comprehend the fact that the deceased one has merely changed locations. Even though we can no longer see them with our natural eyes, they have not ceased to be!

For we fix our eyes not on what is seen, but on what is unseen, since what is seen is temporary, but what is unseen is Eternal (2 Corinthians 4:18 NIV).

Chapter 6

Three Angels

For You formed my inward parts; You wove me in my mother's womb. I will give thanks to You, for I am fearfully and wonderfully made (Psalm 139:13-14).

Open heart surgery is any type of surgery where the chest is cut open and surgery is performed on the muscles, valves, or arteries of the heart. According to the National Heart, Lung, and Blood Institute, coronary artery bypass grafting is the most common type of heart surgery done on adults. During this surgery, a healthy artery or vein is grafted to a blocked coronary (heart) artery. This allows the grafted artery to bypass the blocked artery and bring fresh blood to the heart.

Charles Haines[3] was recovering from open heart surgery performed two days earlier. He was lying in a hospital bed and a dozen thoughts were rushing through his mind. He was apprehensive about his present physical condition, comprehending that he had a serious problem and knowing some of his issues were not curable by surgery.

Just prior to his surgery, Charles had actually died in the emergency room and was clinically dead for a very brief period. Fortunately, the medical team had been able to resuscitate him and restart his heart. That incident landed him in an emergency surgery. He was very blessed to be in a great hospital with skilled and experienced surgeons caring for him.

3

Charles was keenly aware of his present blessings and he felt certain that God was working on his behalf. Thoughts about life, death and life after death were swirling in Charles' mind that evening. He was troubled to say the least. He had accepted Jesus as his Savior as a young man, but he still had many questions. He longed for some kind of confirmation from God regarding the status of his eternal Salvation!

Suddenly, Charles caught sight of something strange in his peripheral vision and to his right, toward a window. A large globe of brilliant white light projected itself right through the glass window pane into Charles' room! The shimmering sphere of light resembled a large oval globe and it stopped near the foot of his bed. A woman wearing a radiant white robe literally stepped out of the sphere and stood to her full height. She looked like an ordinary woman except for the brilliant white light that meshed with her very being. The light surrounding her gave her a constant glowing appearance at all times!

Charles was startled speechless as he watched the manifestation! The angel stepped forward, looking directly at him. He did not need a news flash. Charles instantly knew he was in the presence of an angel! Without hesitation, the angel began to speak to the patient.

The angel said to Charles, "I know you have had doubts in the past and I have come to reassure you of two things. First, God is real. Second, you are going to be healed and you will make a full recovery." Charles was shocked by the Heavenly revelation in part, because quite honestly he was in a great deal of physical pain. He thought he might be close to death! After all, his chest had been split open two days ago! Also, her words were sobering because she was obviously able to read his thoughts correctly. Without further communication, the woman diminished in visual appearance and was absorbed by the light, just before it traveled back through the window from whence it emerged and disappeared. Charles was understandably in a state of awe and amazement!

Three more days went by. While Charles was alone and lying quietly in bed, the same large sphere of bright white light appeared for a second time! Once again it came through the window glass, proving its ability to move about unhindered by and in spite of material things, as if material things were insignificant. This time, two angels stepped out of the bright light! One was the same angel that appeared days before and the second angel was a male angel.

Charles directed his question to the female angel asking her why the male angel came to see him. She replied, "He is here to see another patient. I brought him with me to reaffirm everything I told you before; so that you will know that my first visit was genuine and everything I told you before is true and factual." She then told Charles they had to go, and immediately both of them dissipated as if they were absorbed or consumed by the shimmering sphere of white energy!

Only hours later, Charles was moved into a regular room and his physician visited him there. The two men discussed the angel visitations. The doctor was not shocked at all, saying he had heard of many supernatural experiences related to his patients and other patients being cared for by his colleagues. That was an extraordinary time of enlightenment for Charles, and his faith in God became stronger as a result of what he had gone through!

When Charles left the hospital he carried his faith with him and he spoke openly to others about his experiences. He was surprised when he learned of others who had firsthand knowledge of similar supernatural manifestations. He entered a conversation with his pharmacist one day when he went to pick up some of his medication. The woman told him a fascinating story!

The pharmacist described how she lost control of her car one evening while traveling on a busy road. The car left the pavement and flipped upside down. The smell of gasoline was in the air. The woman realized she was literally hanging in the car suspended by her seat belt.

She was disoriented and fearful that the car would burst into flames! She went on to describe a sphere of light that appeared just outside her car! She said an angel emerged from the light as if the light took shape and changed into the angel. The angel reassured her that the car would not catch fire and told her that help was on the way! The angel disappeared and momentarily a Good Samaritan who stopped after seeing the wreck arrived and freed her from the seat belt and pulled her from the wreckage.

Two weeks later, Charles delivered a Christmas basket to an old friend he had not seen in a very long time. There is just something about coming so close to death that makes you want to treasure family and friends you might have taken for granted before. The old friend, Roger, was glad to see Charles and eagerly listened to his angel stories, then shared his very own After-Death-Appearance with Charles!

Roger told of a time when his brother was dying from cancer. He was a patient in a hospital at the time. Roger was overcome with emotion and exhaustion, so he decided to go home and get a good night's sleep. He spent a fitful night sleeping little. Early the next morning, his wife went into the kitchen leaving him in the bedroom alone.

Suddenly a sphere, an oval shaped globe of white light the size of a small cantaloupe appeared in the darkened bedroom! It came right through the wall and flew around the bed several times before it soared away by traveling through the wall as it continued on its way! Roger intuitively knew the light was his brother! Only minutes later a nurse from the hospital called to tell Roger that his brother had just died! Roger said he was not surprised at all because while the After-Death-Appearance was in progress he was acutely aware that his brother was in the fast moving ball of energetic white light!

Stories abound about "Natural-Supernatural" Appearances and "Ordinary-Extraordinary" Visitations. The experiences are incredible. However, they are very natural occurrences and wide spread. Most people are hesitant to tell others what they have seen or experienced. I am happy to learn that many people are opening up and realizing their experiences are not abnormal but very normal indeed! God Himself causes these hope filled manifestations and we should be quick to offer Him praise, honor and glory for His tremendous gifts!

Chapter 7

Unspoken Words

Blessed are those who mourn, for they shall be comforted (Matthew 5:4).

After-Death-Appearances don't always come in the forms we might expect, yet still they are genuine! Mrs. Emily Wilson[4] discloses about her experiences that began to manifest in the first few weeks following the death of her middle-aged husband, Thomas. At first, she had a dream of her deceased husband in which he was silently motioning for her to follow him. They ended up at either a utility pole or telephone pole. The deceased lifted a large roll of wire and he began pulling the wire, stringing it from one pole to the next. Telepathically he conveyed to his wife that he was setting up lines of communication so they could stay in touch. That was all there was to the dream.

The Wilsons had two much loved grandchildren with whom they had spent much of their time since they were babies. Both grandsons were under the age of ten when they lost their grandfather and they had a hard time accepting the fact that he was gone and never coming back. The pain was more than they could handle. Instead of tears, many times they demonstrated their grief through frustration and anger. They raised their voices and cried over insignificant matters because they did not know how to express the grief they were feeling. Help was on the way, although they never could have imagined the way in which it would come!

4

It all began one Friday night as Mrs. Wilson finished reading a story to the boys. Almost immediately she encouraged them to get ready for bed. The boys were reluctant and somewhat rowdy! When the clock struck ten, a loud noise in the form of static came from a radio that was turned off. The static was very loud and it got everyone's attention although they did not know what to make of it! The boys calmed down at once! Mrs. Wilson proceeded to tell the boys they would need to get out of bed by six o'clock the next morning because she had planned some activities for them.

At exactly six o'clock the next morning the loud static noise radiated from the otherwise quiet radio. It was as if an alarm clock had been programmed to sound at a certain time! The following night and next morning, the same occurrence happened again. At 10 p.m. and at 6 a.m. the loud static noise blurted out from the silent radio calling everyone's attention to itself as if to say, "Look at me! I am here with you!" Those occurrences became routine, repetitive, and happened for several months!

The grandmother and the grandsons came to expect the static as a welcome guest! At night time, the boys would respond to the static by saying "Goodnight Gramps!" In the morning time, the boys responded by saying, "Good morning Gramps!" The static was expected every time the little boys came to visit their grandmother.

Once when the younger boy was sick with a sore throat and cough, Mrs. Wilson gave him a dose of cough medicine before she put him to bed. She set the clock for 2 a.m. to awaken her in time to administer another dose of cough medicine. Later on, she realized that setting the alarm wasn't necessary at all! Just moments before the clock alarmed, an unusually loud static noise squawked through the radio speaker into the quiet room, alerting her it was time to get up and medicate the child! Those times of static blasting into the room came to be accepted and recognized as After-Death-Appearances from Thomas, and they were greatly appreciated.

During those unusual weeks, the static persistently interrupted phone calls. As time went by, Mrs. Wilson and others riding in the car with her admitted they too heard the static noise coming from the car radio when it was turned off. The static made known its presence especially when the two grandsons were traveling in the car with their grandmother!

A time of celebration describes the mood during those visits! If the boys were excited and chattering at the same time about a joyous circumstance then the static chimed in over and over again until the boys acknowledged the activity, laughing and saying "hello" to Gramps! The first Christmas Gramps was gone was the most active time for the visits demonstrated by the static noise, and it actually made the season more joyous because the deceased grandfather seemed to be very present and merely out of sight!

In closing, it is difficult to explain what we do not understand. It is impossible to deny what we have most certainly heard with our own ears. Suffice it to say, The Holy Bible declares in Isaiah 55:9, "For as the Heavens are higher than the earth, so are My ways higher than your ways and My thoughts than your thoughts." The wise thing to do perhaps is to just say, "We are most thankful to You Lord for Your marvelous gifts!"

Chapter 8

Rebecca's Heavenly Gift

Love never fails (1 Corinthians 13:8).

Larry Campbell, of Fairview, Tennessee, was only 42 years old when he had a massive heart attack. He was standing on a ladder, sanding a door frame and making it ready for a coat of paint. He did not cry out in pain before he drew his last breath. He did not speak to either of the workmen standing nearby, indicating to them that he was about to fall to the floor! He had no warning. His heart just stopped beating and his life ended.

Consider this; on Judgment Day, Larry will be judged by God, graded on his conduct and assigned to his eternal home based on the condition of his soul when he drew his last breath on March 2, 2002. He had no time to make amends, change his habits, and ask forgiveness or to make a life-changing decision. It was like a 3 o'clock school bell rang signaling the day was done. Time was no more for Larry Campbell. That reality is sobering!

Behold NOW is the acceptable time, behold, NOW is the day of Salvation (2 Corinthians 6:2).

Larry's wife, Mary and their two daughters, Rebecca and Bridgette, were left behind and confronted with the absence of his love and presence; their loss was devastating. They managed to go on because they had the assurance that the husband and father had been "saved"! They were comforted by that knowledge, believing he had entered into Heaven to be with the Lord forever!

Larry's daughter, Rebecca, was in high school at the time, and she was shocked when her boyfriend, Jeremy, ran to her that tragic day, saying something had happened to her dad! He drove her to the hospital and she thought it was odd that he never looked at her, even once during the drive to the Williamson County Medical Center in Franklin, Tennessee.

When the couple arrived at the hospital, Rebecca saw her mom sobbing uncontrollably; Rebecca realized Jeremy knew all along that her dad was dead and just didn't have the heart to tell her. Larry was so young; his death was sudden and unexpected, leaving his family in a state of shock!

That same day, when Larry's mom, Fran Braddy, learned of her son's death, she tragically suffered her own heart attack! She was at the hospital and nurses carried her into the room next to the room in which Larry's body lay cold and motionless. Only a curtain separated the two of them. After an examination, the emergency room physician arranged for Fran to undergo a cardiac catheterization. The procedure revealed a 95% blocked artery leading to the heart, and it was life threatening.

The abnormal medical condition necessitated the placement of a stent to correct the defect. A stent is a small metal mesh tube that acts as a scaffold to provide support inside the coronary artery. A balloon catheter, placed over a guide wire, is used to insert the stent into the narrowed coronary artery. Once in place, the balloon tip is inflated and the stent expands to the size of the artery and holds it open. The balloon is then deflated and removed while the stent stays in place permanently. Over a several-week period, the artery heals around the stent. Fran's procedure produced an excellent life-restoring outcome!

Larry's death caused his mom's heart attack. That sudden crisis led the doctors to discover a life-threatening condition that was correctable if immediate action was taken! One life was taken; one life was spared! A son's death granted life to his much loved mother! It was a very sad day, yet a miraculous one, depending on one's perspective!

Later that same eventful evening, as Fran lay resting quietly, her deceased son, Larry, supernaturally and miraculously materialized before her there in the hospital room in the form of an After-Death-Appearance! She only saw his face as if looking into a round window surrounded by a fuzzy frame. Larry smiled at his mom then spoke, saying, "Mom, I am okay! Please be strong for the girls!" He was obviously referring to his wife and two daughters! Fran was a woman of strong faith. Larry's family would need her to get through the days ahead.

The next three years were sad times; still, life went on as life does. Rebecca married her high school sweetheart, Jeremy, and gave birth to their daughter, Aubrie, in September 2005. Three days after Aubrie was born, Rebecca was home alone with the baby early one morning. She had placed the sleeping infant down on the bed beside her. Sadly, she longed for her dad; Rebecca loved him dearly! The new "momma" wished her daddy could have seen his granddaughter; he would have loved her so much!

At that moment, she heard the front door open and close; that surprised her. She assumed her husband had forgotten something and returned to get it. Rebecca looked toward the bedroom door and was shocked to see a shoulder, and it took her several seconds to determine what it was that she was seeing! Then to her delight, the bodily form of her deceased father emerged from behind the adjacent wall!

What happened next was most unusual, but entirely comforting as it all unfolded. The deceased man, wearing a brown plaid shirt and khaki pants, slowly approached his daughter and granddaughter. Strangely, Rebecca would not be able to feel her father's touch; however, she was able to watch what happened from a distance. The stunned young woman found herself, as if she was out of her body, standing by the dresser, watching!

The part of her brain that could think, see, and hear had been divinely displaced from her earthly body. Larry leaned forward and drew the still upper torso of his daughter toward him then he placed a fatherly kiss on her forehead! He proceeded to pick up the baby; the grandfather held her tenderly as he kissed her little forehead, seemingly in reverence! It is hard to describe the tenderness that the deceased man expressed by his actions. Holy is the only word that describes what took place in those brief and treasured moments!

Rebecca was astounded because her dad's earthly features were familiar, but he possessed so many enhanced characteristics! Larry's face was even more handsome than before and altogether lovely. His blue eyes were more beautiful than before he died; they were crystal clear blue and sparkled with shimmering light! His teeth were radiantly white; they glowed! Larry's entire appearance was perfect and his demeanor was stately! Rebecca knew her dad had been changed by his exposure to the Most Holy God in Heaven! When Larry returned the infant to the soft bed, he promptly vanished, and Rebecca was instantaneously restored to her body. It all happened very quickly.

Rebecca was absolutely amazed by what she witnessed that day! Peace washed over her as she realized her dad had not missed out on all their life events; especially Aubrie's birth! Somehow, God in His splendor, power, mercy and love had caused miracles to abound! He made it all possible!

The After-Death-Appearance that God allowed Larry to make was the most extraordinary gift Rebecca had ever received, except for her new born "angel" Aubrie! To this very day, the episode stands as a testimony of God's limitless power and His incredible love for His children, for those who believe in Him and serve Him in obedience!

> *If you love Me, you will keep My commandments* (John 14:15).

Chapter 9

A Thanksgiving Message

For I will turn their mourning into joy, and will comfort them, and give them joy for their sorrow (Jeremiah 31:13).

Ruth Ann Kelley and her husband, Don, of Bellville, Ohio, were about to celebrate their 40th wedding anniversary. Then, a short time before they reached that mile-stone, Don suffered a massive stroke. He survived it; however, it changed him in many ways. He recovered to the point where he could physically take care of his own needs and he could even drive a car, but the stroke affected his ability to make wise decisions. His mental reasoning was impaired.

For the next 13 years Don's overall health declined. Health problems plagued him as never before. In October of 2009, Don entered the hospital and his family understood that he was living out his last days. When Don left the hospital that time, Hospice nurses assumed his care, allowing him to remain at home for the time he had left.

The day before Ruth Ann took Don home, a surgeon came into the hospital room seeking her permission to do an exploratory surgical procedure on Don. However, Ruth Ann and Don's attending physician both agreed on one thing; Don had been through enough suffering and an exploratory surgery would have been cruel and inhumane treatment. Ruth Ann refused to give her permission and that displeased the surgeon who wanted to perform the procedure, but she stood her ground by saying "no."

Don was taken home on a Tuesday and he died the following Friday morning in his own home with Ruth Ann lying on the bed beside him, and his loved ones in the room with him. It was a holy time for the Kelley family. Ruth Ann made every decision pertaining to her husband just as she believed he would have wanted her to do. Still, the days that followed were very sad times for Don's family.

Thanksgiving Day came a month later and Ruth Ann found herself questioning her own decisions, asking, "Did I really make the right decision about the exploratory surgery? Could that possibly have helped him?" That holiday was a sad time, for it was the first holiday in over fifty years of marriage that Ruth Ann had experienced without Don. She was driving alone on her way to her son's home when she spoke to her deceased husband saying, "Oh Honey, I didn't even give you a chance by allowing them to operate on you."

At that precise time, her deceased husband made his presence known! In his usual voice, speaking clearly and concisely, Don spoke out loud to Ruth Ann saying, "Oh Sweetheart, you did give me a chance! You gave me a chance to die at home with you by my side, my family all around me, not in pain in the hospital! You did give me a chance!"

Ruth Ann could scarcely believe her ears, but she knew full well that she just heard the audible voice of her husband! She was amazed to know that God had allowed Don to realize her concerns; then He allowed Don to address those concerns by speaking in an After-Death message to her!

Ruth Ann never felt guilty again! She leaned on her self-assurance and was confident that she had done the right thing for Don. She knew Don was in God's hands for eternity and his spoken message to her was one of the greatest gifts she had ever received! For sure,

Don was at peace and on that first lonely Thanksgiving Day, God brought Ruth Ann to a place of perfect peace.

> *Thou wilt keep him in perfect peace, whose mind is stayed on Thee* (Isaiah 26:3 KJV).

Chapter 10

The Conversion

If you do well, will not your countenance be lifted up? And if you do not do well, sin is crouching at the door; and its desire is for you, but you must master it (Genesis 4:7).

Jason Ligon was the miracle child born to Wayne and Linda Ligon in Lebanon, Tennessee 8 years after they were married. Linda literally prayed him into existence! For the longest time it seemed like the couple would be childless, but all that changed in the summer of 1986. The long awaited baby boy brought more sunshine into the lives of others than anyone could ever have imagined! Wayne worked for the Corp of Engineers and his work caused him to travel a lot. He was away from home much of the time. Thankfully, there was extended family nearby to fill the void in his absence. Five years after Jason was born, baby sister Courtney came along and the Ligon family was complete!

Jason's maternal grandmother, Granny Bennett, was well up in years when Jason came along. That sweet and gentle lady gave birth to her son a couple of months after her first husband was killed in battle in World War II. She married a second time in 1951 to Edward Bennett and they had one child, Linda, who was to become Jason's mom. At the age of 14, on one hot August day, Linda watched her father die of a massive heart attack on their front lawn. Mrs. Bennett was widowed a second time. She remained single and earned a living working in a floral shop.

Jason's birth signaled a much needed interval of happiness for Granny Bennett and she took advantage of the opportunity! The newborn belonged to Granny Bennett as much as he did to his parents! From the time he could walk, Granny Bennett dressed Jason up in his finest clothes on Sunday mornings. She would stand him on a church pew, pin a rose boutonniere on his lapel and then tell him he looked "dapper."

Bennie and Ernesteen Ligon were Jason's paternal grandparents. The two of them loved Jason immensely. Granddaddy and Granny Ligon played a huge part in Jason's upbringing and the way in which his life progressed. While growing up, Granddaddy Ligon was young Jason's hero and best friend. Their special love has not diminished with the passing of time.

Granddaddy Ligon had many siblings and Jason loved all of them. However, Uncle Hut stood out in the crowd! Uncle Hut could run like the wind! Running at full stride he could catch a rabbit with his bare hands! He could tell if a young boy was growing normally by counting his ribs! When Uncle Hut counted Jason's ribs it was merely an excuse to tickle him mercilessly until he laughed hysterically!

When Jason was only 4 or 5 years old, he spent most Friday nights in the home of Granddaddy and Granny Ligon. The youngster filled up on bacon, eggs, and biscuits early on Saturday mornings while anticipating the arrival of Uncle Hut. Uncle Hut would show up and whisk Jason away in his old black pickup truck. They would head straight to Carthage to the stock yard. The nearly 30 minute drive was spent talking about the "good old days" when Uncle Hut and Granddaddy Ligon were young boys going on cattle drives to town. Oh how those stories made Jason's eyes light up! He wished he could turn back the hands of time and be a part of those days gone by!

As they neared Carthage, Jason's anticipation swelled while his eyes peered over the dashboard! There was the infamous Carthage Bridge in Smith County and crossing it always made Jason shiver! Poor "fella"! He learned to close his eyes, hold his breath, and pray until they safely reached the other side! The bridge was rickety at best! Soon enough, they would come to the stock yard where the parking lot was filled with old worn out farm trucks with muddy tires and huge livestock trailers in tow.

Near the barn entrance sat an old man selling cedar sticks for whittling. Uncle Hut gave in one Saturday and bought Jason a cedar stick. Jason took out his Old Timer pocket knife then tried his level best to sit, whittle, and spit on the ground like the old men did. The young boy mimicked their moves and small talk, trying to be one of them! Cattle days with Uncle Hut were some of Jason's best days!

Growing up in Lebanon provided simple, happy, and heart-warming memories for Jason. Granny Bennett was the oldest of ten children, nine of which were girls. Jason spent time with all of those great aunts and each one tried to become his most-loved aunt by cooking his favorite foods, playing his chosen games, and making him feel dearly loved in every way possible!

Jason's grandmothers and aunts were all excellent cooks and no matter when he arrived in one of their homes, food was cooking or waiting for him. There was the smell of delicious yeast rolls, cakes, pies, fried chicken or chicken and dumplings swirling in the air! How could he be anything but happy when everything tasted so good and where everyone loved him so deeply!

As a small boy, Christmas time was perhaps the most special

of all times! Christmas encapsulated so much joy! On Christmas Eve, Granny Bennett would drive up in her little old 1978 brown Chevrolet Impala. The car would be loaded down with food she had painstakingly prepared, keeping in mind everyone's preferred dishes! They would load all the gifts into the car, along with themselves, and head out to meet the rest of the gang!

Members of Jason's extended family were so numerous that no one had a home large enough to hold them! They were accustomed to gathering at a Lodge near Lebanon on Christmas Eve where everyone brought food and visited until late at night. The smell of good food, the laughter and sincere joy expressed by a loving family rejoicing over being together while celebrating the Lord's Birthday, was too perfect for words! The season always passed too quickly.

While some kids were out running the streets, Jason was growing up surrounded by elderly people who saw the value of mentoring and loving him. Since his mom was a church pianist, he spent much time listening to the choir singing sacred hymns. Entertainment consisted of watching Mr. Ed and The Andy Griffith Show on television. When Jason was 9 years old, the time came for a summer revival at Fairview Baptist Church. Although he had been brought up in the church, the child really had no clear concept of what it meant to be "saved." The same is true for most children. It is extremely rare for a young child to experience genuine Holy Spirit conviction to the point of actual conversion. How wise are the adults who acknowledge this truth and act accordingly on behalf of innocent and immature children.

The Spirit Himself testifies with our spirit that we are children of God (Romans 8:16).

One night at revival, Jason watched his friend go to the front of the church at the end of the preaching service to get saved and he envied the attention his friend received from the congregation. Strangely, he felt a little sad and a little jealous that he was not getting the same attention. Jason thought to himself, "Maybe that is what we are supposed to do as people who go to church and try to live good lives. If walking to the front is all it takes to get saved well, that's not so hard."

He went home that night and his mother, in sincerity, read him some Scriptures from the Bible. Then she led him in the Sinner's Prayer and he repeated the words after her, but he felt no different than before. A short time later, he walked the aisle, repeated some words after the preacher, and then the preacher told him he was saved! Everyone congratulated him and he wondered why he waited so long. It was such an easy process of simply reciting a little prayer. Jason really thought he should feel differently, but he felt the same.

Time passed and Jason graduated from High School. He was working at Edward's Feed Mill just off the Lebanon City Square when he was confronted with going to college or working at the mill indefinitely. He considered his options. Ligon and Bobo Funeral Home was next door to the flower shop where Granny Bennett worked. Jason's family actually started that Funeral Home back in 1920. As a child, Jason had spent many days going back and forth between the two businesses and the place fascinated him; it had for a long time. He liked the funeral directors and admired the way they lived and the way people looked up to them.

Jason aspired to become a Funeral Director and Embalmer, so he enrolled and ultimately graduated from John A. Gupton College in Nashville in 2006 with an Associates of Arts Degree in Funeral Services. A two year apprenticeship was required after college in order to get a Funeral Director's License. That requirement led Jason to Gallatin, Tennessee where he began his apprenticeship. After working for three years in Gallatin, he accepted a position in Lafayette, Tennessee and after moving there, he settled into a small apartment above the funeral home.

Lafayette was the one place Jason had never wanted to live. However, it was where God sent him for specific reasons. Soon after he started work, the owner drove him to a local bank to open a new bank account. Jason's boss introduced him to the bank manager whose daughter introduced Jason to her best friend, Amie. The two were well suited for each other. Jason was smitten with that lovely young lady from their first encounter! Amie's love, faith, and prayers would prove to be extremely beneficial to Jason in the days ahead. Their meeting was a divine appointment!

Jason began attending church with Amie at Enon Missionary Baptist Church where Amie's family had worshiped for many generations. It was unlike any service he had ever attended. People stood up praising the Lord out loud during the service. They raised their hands in the air, testifying unashamedly, and in Jason's mind the noise was distracting! The piano was out of tune and at times the singing was off key! Having said all that, he felt the presence of the Holy Spirit in that little church; it was most unusual and very interesting!

Before long, that same church held a summer revival. During one of the services, the brother of Jason's boss got genuinely saved! Everyone at the funeral home was overjoyed the next day. There were tears and laughter in celebration of the joyous occasion! Jason heard all the commotion and for reasons he could not explain, he was offended. His emotions were similar to those he experienced when he was 9 years old. Unanswerable questions resurfaced in him and a spiritual battle unlike anything he had encountered, erupted in his life!

Later that day, Jason stood thinking some deep thoughts while pumping gas into the tank of his car. He clearly heard the Lord speaking to him in the same way an ordinary man would have spoken.

The Lord said, "You know you are lost don't you? You know what I have been trying to tell you and show you this past week; and for many years now! What will I have to do to you to make you see if you were to die today, you would spend eternity in hell!"

That Divine message was honest and sobering! It affected Jason in a powerful way!

Jason was compelled to call his boss when he got in the car, asking the man to pray, saying he was not sure where he stood with the Lord. Jason's boss, a mature Christian, agreed to pray. He also called all of his employees asking them to pray for Jason. The wise man realized Jason was lost and in the midst of a spiritual battle. The fight over Jason Ligon's soul was in progress and he needed all the prayers he could get!

Later that evening Jason, Amie, and her mom went to the revival service. Jason's spirit was in turmoil; he was feeling angry and confused. The sermon was seemingly preached solely for his benefit. He knew God was reaching out and calling him to repentance.

Still, there was the lingering question Jason kept asking himself; "What happened to me when I was 9 years old? I thought I was saved then!" He realized he had been deceived at that young age and the knowledge bothered him. How could he have believed so wrongly? Didn't the adults involved realize his childish insincerity; didn't they know that without a change of heart there is no conversion? Why did they not tell him the truth; were they deceived as well?

The church walls began closing in on Jason! One urgent thought topped all others; Jason had to get out of that church! He faked a phone call, exited the building and ended up in a cemetery adjacent to the church property. He walked every row of graves talking to an imaginary person on his cell phone. The pretense continued until service was over at which time he and his little entourage drove away.

Jason, Amie, and her mom rode home in silence. Amie's faith had been tested and strengthened the year before when her dad was killed by a powerful tornado when it stormed through Macon County. She comprehended the certainty of death and the need to live each day as if it was the last day. Amie saw no reason for Jason's procrastination. It bothered her although she kept her feelings private. She knew God would change his heart if she would not give up on him, so she prayed more persistently than ever before!

Jason dropped Amie and her mom off at their home and drove to his apartment. He bounded up the stairs to his apartment above the funeral home in search of familiar surroundings seeking a sense of normality. A slow drizzling rain was steadily falling by then and thunder rumbled in the distance.

Sleep would not come easily that night. Jason wrestled with God and with Satan. He felt like two dogs were fighting to the death in his inner being! Angrily, he questioned God, saying, "God, I thought You saved me that night when I was a kid!" Silently, relentlessly and persistently, God continued convicting Jason's heart, drawing him ever closer to Himself.

Hell was too terrible to imagine for more than a moment and Jason knew what he had to do to get right with God. There was a terrible evil force inside influencing Jason and pulling his heart away from God each time he leaned toward God. Jason washed his face, trying to clear his mind. He turned off the lights, and climbed into bed. There were usual dim shadows cast across his bed by a streetlight near the building. Exhausted, he drifted off into a restless sleep.

Around one o'clock in the morning, Jason woke up to an eerie setting. His personal space was ordinarily bathed in soft dim light along with a few shadows. To his dismay, it was now shrouded in bone-chilling pitch blackness. There was not one smidgen of light the size of a pin head in the room! He found himself engulfed in complete darkness, then he broke out in a cold sweat. Except for a slight ringing in his ears and the pounding of his heart, there was only an unnatural silence.

The troubled man was intensely aware of an unimaginable evil presence in the room. He intuitively knew that Satan was nearby, wanting him to suffer. He was surprised that he did not hear him breathing. Jason felt the relentless force of evil drawing him into an invisible abyss, winning the struggle; at least for the moment. The hairs on his arms stood up; Jason felt unabated sheer terror!

Jason was convinced that Satan was laughing at him! After all, Satan had deceived him into believing he would go to Heaven because "he was a good little boy who went to church; who didn't drink, smoke or curse." However, that kind of thinking was all wrong. In Jason's mind the truth became distinctly clear.

You don't go to Heaven by being good, going to church, or reciting a cookie-cutter prayer. Deception is straight from hell and Jason had eaten the fruit of lies. As a child, no one told him his heart would be changed if he was actually saved. They should have. No one bothered to explore the truth with him about genuine Salvation and imitation Salvation. Those older and supposedly wiser church-goers were willing to be nonchalant and vague about eternity, hell and Heaven. "Why, for crying out loud?"

> *I tell you, no, but unless you repent, you will all likewise perish* (Luke 13:5).

The hellish time continued. Darkness wrapped Jason in its wings as a sweltering heat burned him up on the inside. He sprang out of the bed, groping for the light switch. The evil force did not leave his presence immediately, even in the light. Quickly, Jason called Amie and asked her to pray for him! His mind was racing and he felt sick!

Amie asked what was wrong. Jason said, "I don't know what is wrong! I don't know what is happening, but something is happening! I can't explain it. Please pray for me!" He was in a "tug -of- war" with God holding one hand and Satan holding the other one.

> *The pangs of death surrounded me and the pangs of Sheol laid hold of me; I found trouble and sorrow. Then called I upon the name of the Lord; O Lord, I beseech Thee, deliver my soul!* (Psalm 116: 3-4 NKJV).

Jason placed the phone receiver in its cradle and left the frightening bedroom. He turned on the television, looking for a distraction to take his mind off the uncompromising God from whom he was running. Eagerly, he watched for the first light of sunrise, hoping it would usher in a new day that would turn out to be an ordinary day like all the rest.

The day came and went. Jason could not focus on his work. He was only able to go through the motions, fearfully aware that danger was pursuing him. Without a doubt he was being persistently hunted by the two most powerful and unyielding entities in the universe!

It was June 25, 2009. That night, Jason returned to the church where Elder J. E. Shoulders was preaching the sermon. Once again, every word of the sermon seemed like it was spoken directly to Jason. The preacher zeroed in on him and although he tried to keep his head down, each time he raised his eyes they met the steady gaze of that man of God in the pulpit! Near the end of the service as the pianist played the song of invitation, the preacher left the pulpit, walking directly toward Jason, without ever breaking eye contact.

Brother Shoulders placed his hand on Jason's shoulder saying, "Young man, are you lost?"

Jason replied, "Yes sir, I am." For the first time, he admitted it!

The preacher replied, "Do you know what you have to do?" After the fact, Brother Shoulders told Jason that the Lord spoke to him during the service, telling him to go to Jason because he was lost.

Jason stepped into the aisle going no further. There he fell to his knees, no longer caring where he was or by whom he was being watched. Nothing in the whole world mattered except getting right with God and being saved at that precise moment! Uncontrollable tears streamed down his face, washing away the past, purifying his heart for the spiritual rebirth of a brand-new born again man!

Jason's future wife, Amie, stood next to him with her hands on his shoulders praying for him as Jason prayed, "Lord, I am a sinner, lost, and without You. Please forgive me for running away from You for so long. I'm sorry. Please redeem me and forgive me for everything I've done wrong! Please deliver me from this cruel evil one that is pursuing me, the evil one I have experienced firsthand! Lord, please save me!"

When it was all over Jason stood up. He was a new creation, the image of his Heavenly Father! He was altogether changed! There was a change of mind and a change of heart! He later remarked, "I was seeing through new eyes, my surroundings had changed. Everything looked different. Neither the room nor the people looked the same! My perception and my perspective had been transformed. It was like I was swimming in God's sweet, holy peace! I was filled with a perfect knowledge that I was in my Father's hands. I was happy to be there. I knew I was going to be okay!"

On July 19, 2009, Jason Ligon was baptized in the Long Fork Creek a short distance from the church in Lafayette. His family and the congregation gathered with him to witness the sacred ordinance. That day was Jason's dad's birthday. After watching his son get baptized Jason's dad embraced him telling him it was the best birthday present anyone could ever have given him!

After Jason's conversion experience God placed his feet on a new path. He had a sincere change of heart along with a strong spiritual conviction to tell others about what happened to him! What is memorable and noteworthy is this: The most definitive characteristic of a truly saved person is that he or she will have a burden for lost souls! It is impossible for one who is saved to refrain from sharing their conversion with others from that day forward! It is a tell-tale sign of authenticity and in the absence of that characteristic, one should question whether or not the conversion experience was genuine or imitation!

Amie and Jason married on November 21, 2009. In May of 2012 the couple moved to Lebanon, Tennessee where Jason now serves as a deacon at Lebanon First Baptist Church. He is employed by Ligon and Bobo Funeral Home as a Funeral Director and Embalmer, a position that providentially came about, seemingly by divine intervention. Jason had aspired to work there since he was a child. When the position fortuitously availed itself, Jason saw it as a gift from Heaven!

Where ever Jason finds himself standing is his mission field. In his chosen profession of dealing with funerals and vulnerable family members of those who have died, he is reminded daily how important it is to live life knowing that today might be the last day. His advice is, "Be ready. Death is a certainty, but if you are truly saved then death is not a frightening prospect; instead it is a pleasing transition!"

> *And I saw the dead, the great and the small, standing before the throne, and books were opened; and another book was opened which is The Book of Life; and the dead were judged from the things which were written in the books, according to their deeds. And if anyone's name was not found written in The Book of Life, he was thrown into the lake of fire* (Revelation 20:12-15).

And in case the above Scripture seems too unbelievable to some, I will, as always, let Scripture be its own commentary, considering one more Holy Scripture:

> *For the message of the Cross is foolishness to those who are perishing, but to us who are being saved it is the power of God* (1 Corinthians 1:18 NIV).

Chapter 11

The Rescue

For He will give His angels charge concerning you, to guard you in all your ways (Psalm 91:11).

Ruby Moss, my dear mother, was living in Durant, Mississippi, when she was diagnosed with cancer of the mouth. Unfortunately, the doctors pronounced a miserable prognosis to her. Without radiation to the head to try and stop the aggressive disease, she would not live long; and even then, her existence would be tortuous. Doctors warned the cancer would grow in size until it left no space in her mouth, making it impossible to breathe, speak, or eat. She readily agreed to receive the radiation treatments, giving no thoughts to the radiation side effects. Losing her memory and ability to smell and taste seemed insignificant considering the alternative.

Over a four week period, Mom traveled to Jackson, Mississippi for radiation treatment every other day. The process was terribly uncomfortable. Finally the day came when she took the last treatment and prepared to wait and see what the outcome would be. Back in the quiet of her home, the elderly widow woman passed much of her time by simply reclining on her bed reading her well-read Bible. She knew her time was short and her earthly life was diminishing each day. Spiritual strength was sought by reading the incorruptible Word of God, and its holy power sustained her in the midst of changes that were most unkind.

Mom's ability to smell soon vanished. She was no longer able to smell the fragrance of flowers, the smell of delicious food or the sweet scent of perfume. All of her ability to taste disappeared. Losing the sense of smell and taste was disturbing! The discomfort of the physical eradication of the cancer was very painful and unpleasant, as she expected. Loss of memory came next. She could remember events from childhood; however, she had trouble remembering the day of the week and where she put her glasses. Her short-term memory was greatly affected.

One afternoon, Mom decided to have a cup of tea. She would not taste it, but she was able to distinguish hot from cold. Holding a cup of warm liquid might be soothing to her nerves, she thought. She placed the kettle over the gas burner. When the steam whistled from the kettle, she removed the tea pot from the stove and poured herself a cup of hot tea. The sad lady retired to her bedroom to rest, carrying her tea cup along with her.

A short time later, Mom jumped up from her chair and ran to the kitchen! Why would she do such a thing? Because she smelled the strong and decisive odor of gas and that smell warned her that she was in immediate danger! A quick look at the stove top revealed one of the knobs was turned on high; however, there was no flame. In her confused state of mind, she must have turned the knob on and left it accidentally. Mom quickly turned the knob off!

When she returned to her bedroom, she sipped some tea from her cup and was reminded once again that she could not smell it. She reached for a bottle of cologne on her dresser and sprayed a small amount on her wrist. She could not smell its wonderful fragrance! How could that be? She certainly smelled the offensive odor of gas leaking from the stove!

A peace settled in her mind all at once, knowing the Lord had sent her protection from a gas explosion and fire only minutes earlier!

The Lord turned on her sense of smell when it was a life or death situation. He evidenced His presence to her and there was no other justification. Mom felt very special and very blessed!

God was watching over her, although it seemed like she was alone in her time of suffering. That amazing rescue from the gas leak and what might have been was a lovely reminder that God loved her up until her death! Mom was cured of the cancer and lived another 5 years, although she never regained her senses of smell or taste. Neither did she fully regain her short term memory. She did live a pain free life and for that blessing, she was outspokenly thankful and praised the Lord for her blessings!

Do not fear, for I have redeemed you; I have called you by name; you are Mine! (Isaiah 43:1).

Chapter 12

Out of Sight, Not Out of Mind

Did I not say to you, if you believe, you will see the glory of God? (John 11:40).

Sandie Cooney sat on the cool green grass staring into the distance. She was very happy the snow had vanished leaving behind a chill in the air and the hope of renewed life in the springtime to come! She smiled slowly, noticing a sprinkling of green leaves in the tall trees along the property line of the cemetery. Twice each year, Sandie carried a bouquet of flowers to place on the grave of her father. It was not her favorite thing to do. However, considering the fact that she was the only sibling still living in Oriskany, New York, the task fell to her. Each visit forced Sandie to acknowledge that her wonderful dad was really dead. Positively, he was no longer living on this earth. She missed him tremendously and the pain was intense at times, even though he had been dead for many years.

Guy Mezza had been an outstanding man of wisdom and integrity. He was deeply loved by his wife Joyce and his three children, Paul, Michael, and Sandie. Guy was born to be a leader, always intuitively knowing the right thing to do and say in every situation. His family depended on him, perhaps too much. They were willing and eager to follow his lead, take his advice, and seek out his good judgment both in small matters and in trying times.

When Guy and Joyce learned he had lung cancer, they were devastated. Guy insisted they should keep the news from their youngest son, Michael, for as long as possible because he was just entering college at LeMoyne University in Syracuse, New York. Mike certainly knew his dad was ill, just not how seriously ill until very near his time of death. Hospice was called in when Guy was nearing the end of his life and the nurses were able to help in many ways.

The time came when Paul's wife, Karen, was celebrating her birthday. The nurses encouraged the family to leave Guy for a little while, hoping they could relax and have some birthday cake as a brief escape. While they were gone, Guy slipped into a peaceful permanent state of rest. Later, the Hospice nurses told Joyce that just because Guy was unconscious did not mean that he could not hear. Apparently, the ability to hear is one sense that remains intact when a person is involved in the life to death transition. Looking back, Joyce believed Guy waited for them to leave that day so that his death might be less painful to them.

Losing the much loved husband and father at the young age of 54 was the most heartbreaking experience the Mezza family had ever known. Still, there was no way around the reality of what had happened, and each one in his or her own way, attempted to accept the cold hard facts and go on with life as well as they could.

Nearly two months had passed when the youngest son, Michael, came running out of his room one night, steadfastly announcing that his dad was calling out his name! In the darkness of his room, Michael did not see his dad, but his voice was unmistakable! Guy's strong voice broke the silence of night as he called out to Michael, wanting to get his attention, making him aware that he had not ceased to exist! Guy's unmistakable voice was all the proof that Michael needed to know his dad had paid him a very real visit even if it was a brief visit!

Sandie coped with her loss but she spent many sleepless nights grieving. Her husband, Jerry, worked during the night, and the aloneness made her time of suffering even more severe. Guy and Joyce had been excellent grandparents to Sandie's three children Jason, Shawn, and Jamie. Jason was the first grandchild so they spent a lot of their time with him, naturally! The devoted grandfather's absence was extremely painful since the grandchildren loved him very much!

Only a few months after Guy's death, Sandie awoke abruptly in the middle of the night from a sound sleep. Sandie was startled at first trying to figure out why she was awakened. She looked around the dimly lit room, then toward the bedroom door. The source of light was better in the hallway and there in the doorway stood Guy Mezza! Sandie could hardly believe her eyes, but there was no denying it! She could not take her eyes off the clearly defined appearance of her dad standing there, silently looking back at his astonished daughter! He looked normal and natural as he did in life. Guy was visible for at least a full minute; he made no attempt to communicate with spoken words.

When this deceased father was sure that undeniable visible contact had been established between Sandie and himself, Guy seemed contented and readily removed himself from sight. He faded away from this world to the next world as if it was a simple and normal progression. No doubts have ever entered Sandie's mind about what happened that night, although she cannot fully explain how and why it happened!

Sandie was pleased with her new found awareness, an undeniable remembrance that her dad cared for her, even on the other side! Obviously he knew she was having an unusually hard time accepting his death. In light of that comprehension, with God's help, the concerned dad found a way to communicate with his loved ones! His After-Death-Appearance left his family with a holy gift, a genuine miraculous occurrence as a tender offering of hope!

After all, Heaven and earth aren't so far apart! Guy lived his life as a Christian and gained Heaven when he died. His After-Death-Appearance remains a source of consolation to this day, although many years have passed since his amazing visit!

Chapter 13

The Robe

He shall cover thee with His feathers, and under His
wings shalt thou trust (Psalm 91:4 KJV).

Maria Triver[5] lay shivering under the covers wishing for an extra blanket. The room was very cold but she was actually too tired to get up and look for one. She closed her eyes tightly, concentrating on a warm beach somewhere faraway, hoping positive thoughts would help!

Maria's husband had passed away two months earlier, leaving her in a situation where she had to work longer hours leaving her exhausted. She was still very sad and somewhat overwhelmed by it all. However, she was not a quitter. She would do whatever was necessary to survive.

Memories of her deceased husband slipped into her mind even when she tried to force them out. Everyone said it would just take some time for her "new normal" to become her ordinary way of life.

The room seemed to be getting colder. She remembered the large, heavy white chenille robe hanging on the back of the bedroom door. It belonged to her husband and she could not bear to think of doing away with it any time soon. The sad woman thought to herself how cozy it would be right now to be wrapped up in that soft, warm familiar robe!

Ten minutes more passed and the reluctant woman realized sleep

---

5

would not come unless she got warmer somehow. She decided to get up and get the robe from behind the door. That would help. As she swung her legs to the side of the bed she quickly realized she had placed her feet on something other than the carpet. It felt like a soft mound of towels although there was nothing there when she got into bed!

Maria reached for the lamp switch. As soon as the light lit up the room, she was surprised by what she saw! That warm and cozy old robe she had envisioned around her body was at that moment strangely beneath her feet! It was as though someone had taken the robe from its storage place, and then carried it to her bedside before releasing it from above. It fell into a mound by the bed precisely where her feet would land when she got out of bed!

The incident brought tears and laughter! Knowing that she was alone in the house left no room for any other reason for the robe placement other than some kind Heavenly being's hand delivering it! Appreciation filled her up!

She knew her husband was the messenger from Heaven, letting her know he was with her for the time being. He even knew her thoughts, it seemed at first. Momentarily, Maria realized it was God who knew her thoughts and He also knew she needed a touch from her loved one who had crossed over to Heaven!

Maria wrapped up in that robe with an attitude of joy she could not have comprehended any other way! Seeing God work and intervene was perhaps one of the most wonderful experiences she could have imagined! With a thankful heart, she entered a sound sleep.

The joy of the LORD is your strength (Nehemiah 8:10).

Chapter 14

A Penny for Your Thoughts

Are not two sparrows sold for a penny? Yet not one of them will fall to the ground outside your Father's care (Matthew 10:29 NIV).

When Mary Taylor's[6] husband of over thirty years passed away, she entered a time of sadness unlike anything she had experienced before. That first year of Mary's single life seemed like an altered state of someone else's life but surely not her own! That would mean the permanent sadness that plagued her days and nights was an ongoing part of her world. Yet all that Mary feared and dreaded was what it was. She had no choice but to own it and deal with it.

On several occasions Mary sensed her deceased husband was with her. When she drove down the interstate alone she felt him sitting in the passenger seat. When she walked the aisles of the grocery store, she sensed he was walking beside her. Although she did not see him in bodily form, her deceased husband began to make his presence known in more realistic ways.

Here is how it worked. A few days after the funeral, Mary walked across a parking lot toward her car and she found three pennies before she reached the vehicle. No big deal; just three pennies. Two days later, Mary entered a doctor's office and approached the sign-in desk. She glanced down and beside her left foot, there was a shiny penny! A couple of days later, Mary drove through a drive-through and ordered a sandwich. She handed the cashier a five dollar bill

6

and when she received her change, she noticed an unusual penny. It looked very old in comparison to the other coins in her change. A closer look revealed it was a 1951 penny. It was her husband's birth year. That is how it began, and Mary came to accept the fact that whenever she saw a penny in a strange place, it was her husband's way of telling her he was visiting her!

One day she climbed into her car, closed the door, and then reached up to the sunroof to adjust the sliding cover. A penny fell from nowhere and landed in the drink holder in the console! The penny landed on its edge, meaning the penny landed standing up! Strangely, it stayed that way until she reached down and took hold of it! Mary smiled knowingly, and drove along her merry way!

Another time, Mary finished shopping in a large grocery store and proceeded toward the main exit. She glanced down toward her right foot and was very surprised to see a penny rolling along beside her! There was no other shopper near her, so she could not figure out how the penny got there. She walked normally for another 25 feet toward the exit and the penny kept its speed and its course, traveling right beside her foot. A groove or track near the lower portion of the door trapped the runaway penny, or perhaps it would have followed her into the parking lot!

The pennies were a blessing to Mary during those early days of transition from being part of a couple to being alone. It was a small thing, but viewed as a holy gift, a valuable and precious reminder that she was never really alone. The pennies reminded Mary of her deceased husband, but the fact that she was comforted translated into certain knowledge that God was evidencing Himself to a grieving woman in the time of her enormous loss. God reveals Himself in all things! We are sure to see Him if only we will seek Him, then believe that the signs we see are His doing.

Chapter 15

Etch A Sketch®

Cast all your anxiety on Him because He cares for you
(1 Peter 5:7 NIV).

Evie Buchanan passed away on her 61st birthday, leaving behind a devoted husband of more than 40 years. Ken was shocked and devastated by his wife's sudden and unexpected death from an apparent heart attack. After one brief trip to the emergency room where Evie was pronounced dead, Ken discovered his life was forever changed. He was not at all prepared for the lonely and painful days that followed Evie's sudden departure and funeral service.

Evie had the privilege of lovingly caring for two of their youngest grandchildren, ages 3 and 4, from the time of their births up until she died. Hoping to lessen the sadness experienced by the two small grandchildren, Ken decided he would give up his part time job working for a newspaper and take over the duties of babysitting. It was a wise decision. Ken enjoyed taking care of the kids and they seemed very pleased to be spending time with him as well!

Nearly eight months went by, but the passage of time did not ease the grief over the loss of the wife, mother, and grandmother. It was a sad and silent time for the little family without Evie around. Ken's daughter arrived one afternoon to pick up her children and she decided to look through some of her mom's clothing before she left. While she was sorting through a closet in a nearby bedroom, Ken began picking up and putting away the toys the children had played with that day.

He picked up several toys before he came to the Etch A Sketch lying on the floor. (An Etch A Sketch is a mechanical drawing toy with a gray screen and red frame. It was introduced to the U.S. in 1960 and became one of the best known toys of that time period.) Ken stopped abruptly, feeling a profound awareness of wonder as he focused on the screen of the toy! He read the words, and a sense of joy overwhelmed him! It was if his deceased wife had entered the room, reminding him she still cared, even though she was no longer present in bodily form!

Ken read the words "Love ya" clearly written on the screen of the Etch A Sketch. Those words were uniquely Evie's words for she routinely used them on her greeting cards to Ken throughout all their years together. Ken asked his daughter to take a look, and she was as amazed as he was! The children were too small to read or write and no one else had been in the play area except Ken and his daughter. Both of them knew it was a message from Evie, sent to offer hope and encouragement to her loved ones!

Ken had once questioned the certainty of life after death. The After-Death message gave him great peace and a new holy curiosity leading him to search for everlasting answers that only God can provide! Two small words offered Ken and his family hope, and the message opened the door for great possibilities in their spiritual lives! It was surely God that revealed Himself through the deceased woman at the precise moment when their hearts and minds were tender and receptive to a demonstration of His mercy and love, creating a time of searching and looking up to Heaven for answers to all their questions!

Seek the Lord your God and you will find Him if you search for Him with all your heart and all your soul (Deuteronomy 4:29).

Chapter 16

Letter from Heaven

Thanks be to God for His indescribable gift! (2 Corinthians 9:15).

Watching her dad lose his 11 year battle with leukemia was a sad experience for Kristen Felentzer of Scottdale, Pennsylvania. When he passed away in April of 2012, she had an unusually hard time getting used to the idea that he was gone forever. It bothered her tremendously that she could no longer pick up the phone and call him. The fact that Kristen could no longer have a conversation with her dad about important issues or even insignificant matters weighed heavily on her mind. Kristen also struggled, not knowing whether or not he was at peace. Each day after his death, Kristen found herself crying out for some kind of sign to let her know that her dad was alright and in a better place.

It was April 18th, ten days after the funeral, when Kristen's mom was watching Kristen's small children in her own home. Her mom was in her dining room when she heard the front door open and close! She called out asking who was there, but heard only silence. Kristen's 10 month old son was playing in a stationary jumper when the door closed, and his attention immediately changed from the jumper to the direction of the noisy door. The baby's facial expressions changed, like he saw someone. He looked toward the door showing much interest, like he could actually see someone standing there. Kristen and her mom both believed the deceased husband, father and grandfather had paid them a visit!

Another week went by and Kristen was sitting in a chair at her desk one morning trying hard to keep her mind on business. The separation from her dad was still so new. The pain and grief were intense. A flashing light alerted Kristen that her paper tray was empty and the printer stopped. She walked to her supply shelf and retrieved a new ream of paper. Next, she removed the wrapper and lifted a stack of pages an inch thick and filled the paper tray.

There in the remaining pages of crisp, clean pages of brand new paper she saw a colored page filled with writing. The page contained writing that was not just ordinary typed words. It also contained some art work consisting of two hands; one hand resting in the other hand on a yellow background. The lines of type were artistically set on the page. It did not resemble a business letter at all. It was a beautiful page and the words made it even more beautiful! That was most unusual, considering she had opened hundreds of packs of paper during her life. She knew she had never seen anything between the pages except more pages of clean white paper!

Tears filled Kristen's eyes when she began reading the words. Across the top of the page were the words "Letter from Heaven." She knew the letter was her sign from Heaven sent by God to reassure her about her much loved father. The letter was dated April 18, 2012, the same date as when the door mysteriously opened and closed all by itself at her mom's house! It was as if her dad came for a visit and left her a letter that day, although it took an additional week for Kristen to get around to opening the ream of new paper in which she discovered the letter! Here is a portion of the letter that spoke volumes to Kristen:

Letter from Heaven

*To my dearest family, some things I'd like to say,
But first of all to let you know, that I arrived okay.
I'm writing this from Heaven, here I dwell with God
above, There are no tears of sadness here, there's just
eternal love. Please don't be unhappy, just because
I'm out of sight, Remember I am with you, morning,
noon and night. That day I had to leave you, when
my life on earth was through, God picked me up and
hugged me, and He said "I welcome you"...*

P.S. God sends His love!

Anonymous

*And now these three remain: faith, hope and love. But
the greatest of these is love* (1 Corinthians 13:13 NIV).

For the rest of the day after Kristen discovered the letter, she could not keep from smiling and thanking God for His tremendous gifts! The visit from one who was invisible, the time when the door opened and closed at her mom's house was the first gift and the letter from Heaven was the second gift! Perhaps she will never fully know how the letter came to rest in the middle of a brand new pack of copy paper, but she will be happy in spite of not knowing how God arranged it! Both gifts were received with an abundance of gratitude!

Chapter 17

A New Body

Every good thing bestowed and every perfect gift is
from above coming down from the Father of lights,
with whom there is no variation, or shifting shadow
(James 1:17).

John White was living in Donna, Texas when his mother passed away at the age of 84. She departed this life as a saved woman, leaving the earth to go and be with the Lord. Approximately 8 years after her death, the deceased woman appeared to John in an After-Death-Appearance.

One night he was sitting in his bedroom, praying, when he became aware of a gleaming white light that had begun to manifest in a corner of the room near the ceiling! The light grew in intensity glowing brighter and brighter! It frightened John at first because he had never seen anything like it! He stopped praying and began watching the light until it changed and he saw his deceased mother appear in the midst of the white light!

She emerged through the wall as if it was not there at all. John was shocked and amazed as he sat there with his eyes fixed on the woman that entered through the ceiling! The deceased woman drifted downward until she reached the floor near the foot of the bed. Her appearance was that of a 25 year old woman, not the 84 year old woman who died a few years back. She was wearing a beautiful shimmering white gown! John remained speechless as he continued to watch the woman!

Mrs. White began speaking normally to John, saying, "John, do you remember how I suffered from the pain in my feet and legs? I no longer suffer because God has given me new feet, new legs, and a new body!"

John was then able to speak and he asked his mom one question and she was able to answer him. He asked her if she had seen his father in Heaven to which she replied, "I have not seen him but I know where he is. Perhaps someday, God will grant me permission to go and visit him." She did not elaborate and John did not question her further.

The deceased woman told John, "In Heaven, there are so many places to visit and so many things to see. It seems like one just never has time to take it all in!"

Mrs. White concluded her conversation with her son by simply telling him it was time for her to leave. She left the room in the same manner in which she had entered it. She ascended to the ceiling where the bright light was and the light received her, for she vanished inside the light. Then the light diminished until it was no more.

As frequently as he tells the story, John reminds himself that he was wide awake and praying when the incident occurred. He was not fully asleep or half asleep but fully awake! He saw with his eyes and heard with his ears, one who had died 8 years prior to the holy manifestation. The After-Death-Appearance was a faith-builder for John, and has proven to be a gift of encouragement to those with whom John has shared his story!

Therefore encourage one another and build each other up, just as in fact you are doing (1 Thessalonians 5:11 NIV).

Chapter 18

Satanic Forces at Work

For our struggle is not against flesh and blood, but against the rulers, against the powers, against the world forces of this darkness, against the spiritual forces of wickedness in the Heavenly places (Ephesians 6:12).

Stephen Rowland was aware of changes taking place, he could not deny it; he could feel it. He changed rapidly in only 4 short years. Before the indoctrination, Stephen had a very sweet and loving disposition. In the days that followed the indoctrination, he developed a cold and calculating mentality. He had little compassion for others; he became extremely selfish and his efforts were intentional, striving for his own self-gratification. Stephen became hooked on pornography and he picked up a vile cursing habit.

There were times when thoughts infested his mind, terrifying thoughts; he imagined watching people being tortured! He actually considered buying the "Faces of Death" video to explore that horrible reality! Thoughts of sexual cruelty barged in at times and even thoughts of killing another person. He never got close to carrying out any of those horrific fantasies, thank God, but it is sobering when one considers the facts. Those mind-controlling thoughts were shrewdly and intentionally implanted inside Stephen's mind, where they were stored and readily accessible for retrieval at a moment's notice.

The plot to destroy Stephen's mind was instigated by one who is evil and despicable. The mission was carried out without recognition or resistance. The Destroyer I speak of has centuries of experience and he is shrewd beyond our comprehension.

> *The thief (Satan) comes only to steal and kill and destroy* (John 10:10).

By now you may be wondering how one arrives at such an evil place as this! You may be assuming that Stephen has been in an awful prison or perhaps he was held captive by a band of ruthless demon possessed torturers for 4 years! If that is what you are thinking, your assumptions are wrong. His indoctrination took place while he was attending an ordinary secular college in Michigan.

Stephen was raised in a loving Christian home and he attended a Bible-believing church in Flint, Michigan while he was growing up. He went to Sunday School every Sunday morning. His beliefs were formed early in life and he believed the same as his family and friends in reference to Christianity. As long as Stephen remained in his own network made up of family, friends and extended church family, his faith remained strong and untested.

When Stephen Rowland entered college, he encountered concepts that were never mentioned in church. Darwinism, evolution, communism; other world religions, books by atheists; secular humanist teachings; New Age beliefs, the sexual revolution scene, the beginnings of the gay "pride" movement; the ridicule of the very notion of a Heavenly Father, Jesus the Son, and the Holy Spirit. Stephen was overwhelmed with the barrage of different world views for which he had no answers and it proved to be a major distraction! He lost his way and fell away from God!

Jesus said, "I am the Way, and the Truth, and the Life; no one comes to the Father, but through Me" (John 14:6).

All those different ideas brought about a mental confusion in Stephen's mind. Remember, God is not the author of confusion! During his college years, Stephen increased his educational learning significantly. At the same time he became the unsuspecting subject of a subtle satanic indoctrination that led him to an opposite conversion experience from Christianity to Atheism.

Stephen said, "Eventually, I went from a mental state of confusion, to a tentative state of agnosticism for about two years, and then finally to outright atheism. My view of the Bible was that it was probably inaccurate. I had quit going to church before entering college and my transformation was nearly complete."

Interestingly, as a child, Stephen actually had a genuine experience with God! He felt His power and love in his soul and he received many answers to prayer! In his newfound atheism, a process had been put into play by the unseen forces of evil. The process was cunningly put into effect; a means of conscience-deadening, a desensitization toward sin, a spiritual-blinding process. Stephen's actual memories of innocence, the sweetness of spiritual love and closeness to God had been expunged by a clever being, and a master deceiver. Satan was making significant progress in his diabolical creation of perhaps a future criminal, an evil one designed for a special leadership role, or a powerful Narcissist.

At home, Stephen's parents noticed the changes. They looked past the new look of his long hair and the black leather motorcycle jacket he was sporting that might have been explained away as normal teen age rebellion. His mother, a devout Christian, experienced a prophetic dream about Stephen, and when she told him the details, instantly, he knew full well that what she dreamed was the absolute truth!

"God has given me a dream about you Stephen," his mom said to him. In the dream she was coming home, pulled in the driveway and noticed some men were carrying a coffin out of their home. In a panic, she ran up to them and asked what had happened. She opened the lid to the coffin and it was Stephen who was lying dead inside. She woke up and knew what that dream meant. God had given her that dream to let her know that her son was spiritually dead. Stephen forced himself to laugh it off, but in private it bothered him a lot. His mom had no way of knowing the terrible thoughts that were continually flooding his mind but she did notice that he was cold and distant.

There was a slow dawning in Stephen's mind that something really "evil" was going on inside of him. At times it felt like an evil presence in bodily form was there in his bedroom getting very close to pounce on him, taking control of him forever! He could not see the demonic creature but he could feel it! But how in the world could that be real if there was no such thing as evil? Psychologists, evolutionists and physicists did not believe in spirits, good ones or bad ones, and certainly not in a Holy Spirit! Stephen surmised that he was an intellectual atheist and an emotional wreck, starting to frighten himself. He wondered, "What am I capable of if these thoughts keep growing! What is the root cause of all that I have become?"

Casting down imaginations, and every high thing that exalteth itself against the knowledge of God, and bringing into captivity every thought to the obedience of Christ (2 Corinthians 10:5 KJV).

About that time he met a girl in a psychology class who was pretty and she seemed interested in him. Casual conversation led to a date, but she insisted that Stephen attend a church service with her. At the same time he had encountered a physics professor that he really admired. The man was very intellectual and very caring for the students. Once, he invited his class to his home and Stephen noticed a picture of Jesus on the cross on his wall. That shocked him. He had come to view intellectuals in the sciences as being mutually incompatible with Christian beliefs. He wondered if there were more people out there like this professor.

The pretty girl in his class sensed that God was starting to deal with Stephen's heart even though he was still unaware. He was questioning the intellectual status quo of one of his professors one day, and that tipped her off. It soon became evident that divine intervention was at work. What could have triggered such a thing? A faithful mother back home praying fervently for her son with no plan of giving up surely caused it! How many times throughout history can the seemingly impossible conversion of a man be traced back to the prayers of one woman, standing in the gap for a loved one!

The effective prayer of a righteous man can accomplish much (James 5:16).

Stephen agreed to attend church services with the girl who had invited him. It was a small church and they sat in the back. The worship service was intriguing to Stephen and the people there seemed to have a real love for God. Members there had actually experienced healing miracles and some even had x-rays and medical tests to back them up. That really rattled Stephen. He thought to himself that they might all be deluded. However, he could actually feel the love, the sore lack of which he keenly felt inside himself. It reminded him of the love he used to feel as a child in church. He was irritated with himself for craving what these people had in their "ignorance."

The preacher gave a sermon unlike the services he was used to hearing as a child. He was used to sermons that were very stern, but this preacher's message was centered around God's great love for us individually. At the altar call, Stephen was suddenly in a state of anguish and conflict inside his mind. He wanted what those people had, but he hated to admit it. He could feel a convicting power dealing with his heart while a selfish evil power was intent on dragging him out of that church as quickly as possible. His hands gripped the back of the pew in front of him. He somehow knew that God was real and that Jesus was really His Son! He wasn't sure how he knew it; he just knew. It wasn't an intellectual decision; it was a supernatural force of love and conviction that was invading his soul. He wanted to go up to the altar, but he was ashamed to do so.

It was then that a strange thing happened. A young deacon fellow at the church silently walked up to Stephen and whispered in his ear, "Steve, I feel that God may have a word for you tonight. He is willing to meet you right here in your pew if you let Him." He turned and walked away. Those words rattled Stephen and he wondered how that man knew what he was thinking! At that moment, he emotionally crumbled.

Suddenly humbled and hungry for God, Stephen asked Jesus to

forgive him for his sins and to come into his heart. What happened next is hard to describe and may well be out of the ordinary. Many folks don't feel anything much emotionally when they receive Salvation, but they start changing slowly as time goes by as they begin reading God's Word. Stephen literally felt a powerful force flooding into him starting at the top of his head and rushing down through him to the tips of his toes! It was pure love and joy!

What had been extinguished in his soul over four years time was suddenly poured back into him in a moment of time! He cried like a baby. It was the most wonderful feeling he ever felt! It was a pure, holy right-with-God-joy! He felt like hugging everyone in the church!

The terrifying thoughts of sexual violence, murder and torture left Stephen for good. He developed rather quickly a compassion for people along with a real appetite for learning more about God through the Holy Scriptures. He became a regular church attender and as the years passed, he became an adult Sunday School teacher. Eventually Stephen Rowland felt the call to go to Bible College. He excelled in his studies at the Bible College. Since then, he has become an editorial writer for his hometown newspaper, writing from a Christian point of view. Stephen has had the opportunity to share his faith with others while teaching many classes and preaching sermons whenever he is called upon to do so. Presently he has authored three Christian books!

Stephen has been left with a deep appreciation for several things: a praying mother, a classmate who took a chance on him and encountering real genuine love through God's people. Most of all; he has been left with a very deep appreciation of a God who never gave up on him even though he had turned his back on God. That's real love.

Stephen's story ends with this important reminder. Because of his prior experiences, Stephen speaks with mature and sound wisdom. He said, "One final note is this: when intellectual arguments fail with atheists, pray for them and most importantly, show love to them. God can work with that in the unseen environs of the human soul!"

What man among you, if he has a hundred sheep and has lost one of them, does not leave the ninety-nine in the open pasture and go after the one which is lost until he finds it? (Luke 15:4).

Many people believe that once you are saved, as Stephen was, it is impossible to fall away from God. Stephen's experience tells us a different story, as does Scripture, time and time again! We must keep the faith and remain on the narrow road until the end if we expect to enter into Heaven for eternity! If we do fall away from God, we must repent and get forgiveness then stay the course.

But the one who endures to the end will be saved (Matthew 10:22).

Note: These are the books written by Stephen Rowland: (1) Twenty Controversial Issues in Christendom, (2) A Few Theological Reflections, (3) Signs and Wonders: From Cessation to Fanaticism-Towards a Balanced Middle.

Chapter 19

The Corn Maze

Now I know for sure that the Lord has sent forth His angel and rescued me (Acts 12:11).

Tracy Galloway and her husband had been married two years when they moved to their new place in Sabina, Ohio. She was a new Christian and every new day revealed fresh evidence proving that God was real and with her at all times. Tracy's husband worked 45 miles away in Springfield and during the work week she missed him very much, especially since they were still newlyweds!

One day Tracy decided to make lunch for her husband then drive to his office and surprise him! Tracy left home heading for a primary road that would lead her to Springfield. First, she would have to successfully navigate all the secondary roads consisting of a network of narrow roads constructed around numerous cornfields. It was literally a corn "maze." It was like the farmers planted cornfields then cut roads right through them for entertainment purposes!

A corn maze is like a giant puzzle that you walk through; only in Sabina, you had to drive through the maze in order to get where you were going. Since the corn is taller than people or cars, it is easy to get disoriented and those who were unfamiliar with the area had been known to get lost while driving even short distances from home.

Tracy felt confident, although she was not absolutely sure that she would be able to find her way out of the still unfamiliar area. Still, she had to try it. It was like a small strange voice was encouraging her to go anyway! The journey began as a simple drive, but after repeatedly making one turn after another, going this way and that way, Trace realized that she was officially lost! She kept driving in circles, and then became frantic after trying ineffectively to find her way out for a long period of time! The dazed woman passed a few houses, but was somewhat uncomfortable about stopping and asking strangers for help.

Finally, Tracy gave up on finding her way out of the maze, so she pulled her car to the side of the road and stopped. She then bowed her head and began to pray for God to show her the way out or to send someone to guide her. As soon as she said "Amen," raised her head and opened her eyes, she saw a white pickup truck parked right beside her! The vehicle arrived there silently and that seemed odd to Tracy! The driver was a non-descript woman who lowered her window, then before Tracy could say a word, the woman asked Tracy if she was lost!

Tracy nodded affirmatively, and ordinarily she would have verbally thanked the woman profusely! It was her nature to be kind, courteous, and mannerly to others. But that day, strangely, she was very quiet and did not even offer a thank-you to the woman!

The driver of the truck asked Tracy where she was headed, and by that time, she was so distraught that all she wanted to do was to go home! The woman instructed her saying, "follow me," assuring Tracy that she would show her the way home! Tracy willingly followed the woman until they reached a stop sign that stood at the entrance to the maze. The woman turned to go to the left while Tracy turned to the right. At that moment, as if on cue, Tracy remembered she had not thanked the woman for her kindness! She quickly reached her arm out the window to wave a thankful goodbye to the woman and looked in her rear view mirror. To her surprise, there was no one there! The road was empty as far as she could see. The truck and the woman had disappeared!

That area was a rural area and the direction the woman was driving had neither houses nor driveways or businesses. She should have been in plain view, but that was not the case. She had literally vanished!

The word "angel" came to Tracy's mind along with the mental picture of a Heavenly white winged angel! Tracy called to mind many miraculous stories she had heard in her lifetime. She knew that all angels did not appear with wings! Some appeared in bodily forms of human beings. There was no other explanation because real people are not able to disappear. Real angels can disappear!

Tracy sighed with relief and voiced a prayer of thanks to God believing whole-heartedly that God had sent her an angel, not only to lead her safely home, but also to strengthen her newly found faith as a Christian! That day, God planted a seed of curiosity in the new Christian! Feeling very much encouraged after the experience, she wondered why all of that really happened. She did not have the answer, but by faith she believed it was God teaching her and drawing her closer to Himself. The angelic rescue was a sweet and Heavenly gift, one that would never be forgotten!

Draw near to God and He will draw near to you (James 4:8).

Chapter 20

Shielded from Danger

*The LORD will protect you from all evil; He will keep
your soul* (Psalm 121:7).

Ellie Barker[7] calmly drove along a busy inner city street one
morning after running some errands. The kids were in school; she
had finished all of her business earlier than expected. Ellie felt very
peaceful as she drove the speed limit of 45 mph. She was west-bound
in the right lane of two west-bound traffic lanes. There were two east-
bound lanes to her immediate left. Only a line of paint separated the
oncoming and ongoing traffic since there was no turning lane in the
middle.

That was Ellie's specific reason for keeping to the right; the
absence of that middle turn lane placed those driving in that left lane
in a precarious position. In the event that one needed to make a left
handed turn, the driver had to signal well in advance, hoping that
no one would rear-end the sitting-still automobile while waiting to
complete the turn.

Being a careful driver had its rewards! Ellie had a perfect driving
record as a result of that cautious behavior. That particular day was
marked by a clear blue sky. The road was level and straight for at
least 500 yards. The only action that might cause a wreck was a
careless driver attempting to make a sudden left turn with little or no
warning to the driver behind him.

7

As Ellie drove in silence, she glanced up looking in her rear view mirror. From behind, a car was approaching and traveling too fast! The driver of that car was not in her lane, but in the left west-bound lane. There would have been no major problem except for the west-bound car traveling in close proximity to her car. With little or no warning, that driver decided to make a sudden left turn!

The speeding car behind the car making the left turn, suddenly had nowhere to go except through the car in front of him or into her car! It all happened amazingly fast, seemingly in a matter of two seconds, although her comprehension of all that was taking place was nearly in slow motion.

At the precise moment the speeding car reached the point of impact, the driver turned the steering wheel to the right, driving the recklessly driven car into her lane. Ellie had no time to pray a long prayer! She had time for one word and that word became a powerful prayer as she cried out, "Lord!"

She watched as the speeding car merged into the right lane directly into and through her car without making one sound. She slowed her vehicle as the fast car proceeded to go through the front end of her car! She never heard the sound of a crash! For a few seconds, she simply could not comprehend what just happened.

Rationally she knew that another car had just hit the front end of her car and the rear end of the car beside her! All of the three aforementioned vehicles continued on without being affected by the silent collision that just occurred. There was no actual crash in the natural world; no earthly impact and no injury as a result of the silent collision! The collision did not happen in an audible fashion or in reality. There was no evidence that could prove an accident just transpired, although this rational woman was absolutely certain of what she just witnessed, having been a part of the crash!

Ellie continued along her chosen route that day with no human explanation for the automobile accident she just avoided. God had supernaturally shielded her from harm; He delivered her in a moment of near destruction!

She is not alone in what she experienced, for dozens of others have claimed similar experiences. It appears this type of silent and non-consequential collision is a common phenomenon. The only way to make sense of it is by faith, believing God intervened and by His will averted the danger; therefore saving the lives of the occupants involved. These incidents, all similar in nature, authenticate episodes of divine intervention, and are most assuredly miraculous occurrences!

The name of the LORD is a strong tower: the righteous runneth into it, and is safe (Proverbs 18:10 KJV).

Chapter 21

A Heavenly Hug

Surely our griefs He Himself bore, and our sorrows He carried (Isaiah 53:4).

Erica Stevens, of Hermitage, Tennessee, was only 24 years old when she lost her much loved mother, Jennice. Jennice was suffering from and being treated for a debilitating disease known as Scleroderma. Her death came more suddenly than anyone anticipated. She actually died from ingesting an improper dosage of one of her regular medicines which interacted with another medication she was taking.

Scleroderma is a chronic disease and the symptoms vary from patient-to-patient. Severity ranges from mild to life threatening. The disease derives its name from two Greek words: sclera meaning hard and derma meaning skin, according to the Scleroderma Foundation. The symptoms of the disease are similar to other autoimmune diseases and it becomes life-threatening when internal organs are affected and no longer function properly.

A short time after Jennice passed away, Erica began recalling some uncommon occurrences pertaining to her mom. She remembered a dream she had nearly 9 months before her mom's death. She dreamed of visiting with her mom in her home. The visit concluded when Erica said goodbye to Jennice in the garage immediately before driving away, at which time the dream continued.

In the dream, Erica was driving along normally when she felt an urge to turn around and go back. At that moment, a police officer in a police cruiser with flashing blue lights pulled her over and by all appearances it was a routine traffic stop. As soon as the officer reached the car in which Erica was sitting, he made eye contact with her, but remained silent.

Without a spoken word between them, Erica intuitively knew he was about to tell her that one of her parents had died. She assumed it was her father who was in poor health, but her assumption was inaccurate. Erica was shocked when the officer slowly shook his head while wearing a sad expression on his face. An uncanny knowing, an extrasensory comprehension manifested during those moments, and Erica knew the police officer was telling her that her mom had died. The dream ended. She was left with an odd awareness that the dream was an indication of things to come. It was a peculiar occurrence.

A week before Jennice died, Erica was in her bedroom getting ready for work one morning, when she was emotionally overcome by a powerful sense of foreboding! Erica sensed it was a premonition and she was nearly certain her mom was about to die. The Scleroderma had not yet progressed to the point of being life-threatening, so Erica did not know what to make of the forewarning that left her so unsettled. Still, the ominous knowledge hung over Erica like a dark cloud of impending doom.

One week later, Erica's apprehension became reality when she learned of her mom's untimely death. The fact that she did not die from the Scleroderma but from an excessive combination of drugs coincided with the premonition and the dream in which Erica sensed her death was not caused by the disease. It made sense to her after the fact. Jennice actually died in the garage where her body was discovered. Erica recalled the dream! In the dream she and Jennice said goodbye in the garage just prior to the drive that was interrupted by the police officer who brought her word of Jennice's death. The dream was prophetic, for the garage was in fact the place where the death occurred; the place of her final farewell.

A couple of weeks after the funeral, Erica met a woman who told her how she had adopted a practice of going to God in prayer, asking Him to convey messages to her deceased loved ones. She suggested that Erica might want to try doing the same. It gave her great peace, just knowing she was still able to communicate in some holy fashion that was acceptable to God.

Erica took the woman's advice and trusted God with some of her own messages for her mom and the ritual was calming! The concerned daughter sincerely wanted her mom to know she was missed and loved! Still, Erica wished she had some sort of real proof that her mom was receiving the messages. She missed her mom so much, and her grief was extreme at times! She desperately needed to hear from God!

The first Thanksgiving without Jennice was anticipated with much anxiety. Erica's apprehension about the holidays without her mom increased as Thanksgiving Day approached. For days Erica had repeatedly reached out to the Lord in prayer asking Him to, "Please give my mom a hug from me and tell her how much I love her!"

On the Sunday before Thanksgiving, a man that Erica barely knew came up to her at church and initiated a conversation with her. He said, "I don't know how you are going to feel about what I have to say, but in my spirit, God is telling me to give you a hug from your mom!" Erica received the message with great appreciation and enthusiasm!

Erica knew at once that God had heard her prayers and He had delivered her messages to her mom! She felt the love of God more strongly than ever before! Not only did God deliver Erica's messages, but He delivered Jennice's message back to her! Erica received confirmation! It was the proof she so earnestly desired confirming that their connection was still very much alive and in existence!

It was God's hand moving on her behalf in His own way and in His own perfect timing! Erica realized she was the recipient of an extraordinary Heavenly gift! Thanksgiving time would never be the same; even the word "Thanksgiving" had taken on a wonderful new meaning!

Enter into His gates with thanksgiving and into His courts with praise: be thankful unto Him, and bless His name. For the LORD is good; His mercy is everlasting; and His truth endureth to all generations (Psalm 100:4-5 KJV).

Welcome Page Ansonia Trailside Cottage Cedar Rur

Reservations / Policies / Contact Information

Canyon Cour

Creekside and Trailside Va
Creek

**Here in the heart of scenic "Pennsylvar
perfectly located accommodations in
the Pennsylvani**

**More than just cabins, each cottage f
bath, electric heat, air conditioning,
telephone, satellite**

Click a tab above or a picture below for n

Ansonia Trailside Cottage   **Cedar Run**

Cott

...try Cottages

...cation Rentals in the Pine ...Valley

...ia Wilds", we offer clean, comfortable, ...he Pine Creek Valley, at either end of ...i Grand Canyon.

...eatures a fully equipped kitchen and ... gas grill, picnic table, fire ring, free ...V and wifi internet.

...ore specific information and availability

...Creekside   **Slate Run Sleepy Bear Lodge**
...ge

Chapter 22

Divine Intervention

Because thou hast made the LORD, which is my refuge, even the most High, thy habitation; There shall no evil befall thee (Psalm 91:9-10 KJV).

Kerry Musgrove[8] was a woman who for many years had made a daily habit of spending quality time reading her Bible and in prayer. Kerry made the Lord her daily refuge and habitation! One day, she drove her mid-sized car out of the driveway and onto the main road, intending to make her way to the freeway. She had promised to meet a friend at a new restaurant for lunch. It was a beautiful spring day!

The weather was around 70 degrees and the warm sunshine was such a welcome sight after the long snowy winter that recently ended. Kerry gave her right turn signal and drove down an exit ramp; facing west at the end of the ramp is where she stopped for a red traffic light. Fast moving traffic zipped back and forth, traveling north and south, in front of her. She sat perfectly still waiting for the light to change to green, at which time she planned to turn left onto the main road that would lead her to the freeway.

Soon enough, the traffic light turned green. Kerry looked left and right, then forward as she routinely did before proceeding at intersections. She was always cautious, even when a green light indicated she was good to go. She saw no sign of danger and no reason for hesitation, so she accelerated with her right foot while the left signal light was blinking.

8

Abruptly she felt the front end of the car nose down to a split second stop! At once she became aware that her right foot was pressing down hard on the brake pedal as an eighteen-wheeler roared past her! It could have been no more than a few inches from her front bumper. The truck was a blur, traveling illegally in the far right lane, barreling around the stock-still traffic sitting at the red light.

It was impossible to tell for sure how fast the truck was moving. Clearly the impact would have landed at the driver-side door. Kerry did not see the truck coming. The truck must have been exceeding the speed limit if he closed the distance from where he was, far in the distance, to the intersection in the few seconds it took Kerry to look to the left, right, then straight ahead before she accelerated. Kerry was terrified at how close she came to death. That type of collision would have crushed her car into a hood ornament for that enormous truck!

At once, a sense of calm and peace flooded over Kerry, replacing the fear, as she realized how God had most certainly shielded her from danger. Her life had been spared. The blessed woman understood that dying was not in God's plan for her that day. If God had placed a marble in His hand, then closed His fingers tightly around it for safe keeping, the marble might well have been compared to the way in which He protected Kerry that Tuesday morning.

The sequence of events advanced through Kerry's brain clearly and concisely. By her own power, Kerry did not move her foot to the brake because she was in the process of accelerating. At that moment before the incident, there was no foreseen danger in either direction. Her mind was fixed on moving forward and to the left into a south-bound lane. There was no reason why Kerry would hit the brakes. Some invisible, undeniable and unknown powerful entity was looking out for Kerry, and it accurately anticipated danger, taking the proper counter-measure! That same wonderful being with supernatural strength moved Kerry's foot in a fraction of a split-second with great force because the brake pedal was literally pressed all the way down as far as it would go.

Who would believe her if she called them up and said, "An angel just saved my life!" The people who were stopped at the intersection clearly saw what just transpired, but after it was over, everyone drove away as if nothing ever happened.

Kerry vowed that she would cause herself to remember God's great act of mercy and kindness! He was looking out for her and He sent an angel to save her life! The way He revealed Himself that day was an incredible reminder that we are never alone. God is watching! That day would stand out in her mind forever!

And surely I am with you always, to the very end of the age (Matthew 28:20 NIV).

Chapter 23

Amazing Grace

Surely I have composed and quieted my soul; like a weaned child rests against his mother, my soul is like a weaned child within me (Psalm 131:2).

Carol Brown is the author of "Speak Lord, Your Servant is Listening," a wonderful devotional book filled with Biblical truths and spirit-lifting Scriptural promises! The book is a favorite of mine, and I go to it often when I need real encouragement! All the words written on those pages are merely reflections of Carol's faith and her heart. She is a talented and lovely woman who has led an interesting life! She was born in Jamaica to British parents. Her father was a pastor and her mother was a teacher. Her family moved to New York, where she lived for 25 years. She has now retired from the business world and lives with her husband, Ed, in Orlando, Florida. Her mission in life is to persuade others to listen for the voice of God. He is always speaking to us and Carol is always listening for His voice! Carol is a dear friend who has graciously given me permission to share some of her memories of how God showed up on some of her "ordinary-extraordinary" days!

There was a time when Carol went to the hospital because she had a case of double pneumonia. The doctor told her that kind of illness at her age could quickly turn into a death sentence. She reluctantly took to her hospital bed, agreeing to receive the treatment her doctor had ordered for her. Physically, Carol was very weak and the persistent cough that had harassed her for many days was literally wearing her out. It kept her from restful and recuperative sleep. The sleep deprivation kept her from healing properly.

It was bedtime and Carol had coughed until she was dizzy. She was lying very still, trying to relax and rest. Weary and out of energy from exhaustion, Carol was suddenly aware of a nurse standing next to her bed, showing a hint of a smile while staring down into her face. Carol fully opened her eyes and when she looked into the nurse's face, the nurse quickly turned and busied herself straightening the covers on the bed. She introduced herself and made small talk as she walked around the small space, tidying up the room.

Looking back, Carol says it is hard to describe the kindhearted woman. What made her memorable was not her external appearance but her gentle spirit. She was just an ordinary person, an older woman who began to "mother" Carol, making her feel very much at ease by speaking kind words with a soothing voice. The attentive woman picked up a hair brush and began brushing Carol's hair gently as she softly sang an unfamiliar song with a lingering melody. Then the nurse hugged her, wrapping her arms around her as Carol rested her head on the woman's shoulder. That amazingly delightful nurse then prayed a simple and exceedingly beautiful prayer as she tenderly rocked her ailing patient to sleep.

The next morning, Carol awoke in her hospital bed with her head once again lying on the pillow. Her thoughts quickly reverted to her last conscious moments from the previous night, when she was sitting upright with her head resting on the nurse's shoulder, listening to that Heavenly prayer! What a deep and peaceful sleep Carol experienced! It was the first night of restful sleep Carol had experienced in many days. She was so thankful for it! She felt strong and completely well again! The doctor came in while making his rounds and was surprised to see that Carol had made a miraculous overnight recovery! He saw no reason to keep her as an in-patient any longer, so he discharged her, telling her to go home and take care of herself!

The next day Carol decided to contact the hospital in order to locate the nurse. She sincerely wanted to find her to thank her for her kindness that came at a time when it was greatly needed. Carol reached the head nurse in charge of the hospital floor on which she was previously confined. Carol provided her with the nurse's name, asking if she could give her a message. The head nurse was hesitant at first, then somewhat baffled. She said she knew all the nurses who worked that floor and no one by that name worked there. Carol then described the woman and learned there was no employee there who matched the description.

In a moment, Carol comprehended what had taken place! She had been cared for by a ministering angel from Heaven, sent to her by the God of Abraham, Isaac and Jacob! Carol's devoted life to God had not gone unnoticed by her Heavenly Father. Therefore, when she really needed help, He saw fit to send help in the form of an angel!

Do not neglect to show hospitality to strangers, for by this some have entertained angels without knowing it (Hebrews 13:2).

Chapter 24

When Thunder Speaks!

The LORD thundered from Heaven; the voice of the Most High resounded (Psalm 18:13).

My good friend, Peggy Culbert from Sewell, New Jersey, called me up one day and asked, "Do you believe God speaks in thunder?" I replied affirmatively, saying I had experienced it personally in the past. She proceeded to tell me how she recently experienced a magnificent manifestation of God's awesome communication and presence!

At the time, she was listening to a song called "Heaven on Earth[9]." When the vocalist reached the line saying: "Lightning and thunder, miracles and wonders, sounds of many waters, Heaven on earth," Peggy was amazed to hear and feel God's vocal presence in a most unusual way!

There was an enormous peal of thunder that rumbled in unison with the music! She called it a "Divine orchestration of God, emphasizing His over-riding power and holy might in the Heavenly places!" I believe she assumed correctly! The Bible teaches us that God communicates by using clouds, rainbows and thunder! Peggy's experience reminded me of a similar experience that I had when God spoke in my presence, also using His magnificent voice of thunder!

It happened on a day when I sat at my small dining room table in my home in Lebanon, Tennessee. I was reading a book that Peggy

---

9

had sent me. The book was titled "Prayers and Promises" by Robert Morgan. I thought it was a significant book because Peggy lives in New Jersey and she felt inclined to buy that specific book at a local book store, and then send it to me in Tennessee. It is a wonderful book; but what makes it so very worth mentioning is the fact that the author of that book happens to be Rob Morgan, the Pastor of a Church in Nashville. He pastors the church of which I am a member!

Peggy and I both knew that her sending the book to me was no coincidence! God was involved in that deed because He knew I was praying earnest prayers for many people who were lost! I needed all the help I could get. God sent me His coveted help through that book!

As I sat there reading, I discovered chapters that were actually prayers made up of Bible Scriptures. Each prayer was uniquely constructed and contained blanks so the reader could insert the name of the person in need. When I read and prayed each prayer, I saw the book as a powerful partner in my prayer life. I knew full well that when we use Scriptures, also known as "The Word" in prayers, those prayers become exceedingly powerful!

In the beginning was the Word, and the Word was with God, and the Word was God" (John 1:1).

A Scriptural prayer is potent. It is like an arrow loosed from a sturdy bow by the strong hand of a skilled archer! The prayer that is constructed of The Word becomes a supernatural arrow traveling precisely to a specific target. An arrow is made up of a head, shaft and fetching. The entire Scriptural-prayer-arrow becomes the embodiment of prayer; a message divinely and strategically guided into the holy hand of Almighty God in Heaven! Now that is a persuasive prayer!

For the Word of God is living and active and sharper than any two-edged sword (Hebrews 4:12).

I saw the potential before me and I acknowledged the truth. God Himself had gifted His help to me through Peggy Culbert and Rob Morgan! I became very excited about spiritual possibilities! I used that book to formulate individual prayers for each person on my list.

One memorable day, I began reading each Scriptural prayer aloud. It was a beautiful summer day; not a cloud was in the sky. My surroundings were very tranquil except for the sound of my own voice. I was using a small digital recorder to document those prayers so that I could listen later and pray them again in the car on long drives.

You can imagine how astonished I was when literally, out of the blue, there came such a loud, prolonged, earth shaking, rumbling peal of thunder that it rattled the window panes! A sudden and brief dowsing of rain followed! I knew God was talking to me about someone and something! It was very significant. The Most High God had spoken!

When it was over, I listened to the tape and was encouraged by what I discovered! When God's thunderous voice sounded, I was praying a prayer for one particular lost soul who was consistently rebellious towards God! For the longest time I have referred to him as "Reluctant Paul". It was at the moment when I spoke his (real) name that the thunder rolled! I was so happy to have the experience recorded!

Why do I believe thunder is one of the ways in which God speaks? Because the Bible teaches us this is true! There are dozens of Scriptures pertaining to thunder but I will mention only three.

A voice roars; He thunders with His majestic voice, and He does not restrain the lightning when His voice is heard. God thunders with His voice wondrously, doing great things which we cannot comprehend (Job 37:4-5).

Those who contend with the Lord will be shattered; against them He will thunder in the Heavens (I Samuel 2:10).

Do you have an arm like God, and can your voice thunder like His? (Job 40:9 NIV).

Days later, I carried my recording to that aforementioned person for whom I was praying and persuaded him to listen. He was not impressed; but I was and I still am!

A wise man is he who listens to counsel (Proverbs 12:15).

Surely the thunder was God's way of letting me know that He heard my prayers that day! How happy I will be when He works favorably in the lives of all those for whom I pray; and He will in His perfect timing!

My friend Peggy and I have much in common, and now, additionally, we have each been blessed to have heard the Lord's thunderous voice speaking!

A friend loves at all times (Proverbs 17:17).

Chapter 25

I Have Healed You

"He sent His Word and healed them" (Psalm 107:20).

The time of year was early autumn. Carol Brown had no suspicion that anything was wrong in her body other than a mild case of indigestion. It was Sunday and Carol was sitting quietly in the congregation when the worship service began. The choir was singing "Behold the Lamb" and honestly, Carol found herself a little distracted. She had not transitioned fully into that worshipful frame of mind.

Suddenly, like a swirling blanket of invisible warm sunshine, the Holy Spirit made His presence known! He wrapped Carol in a wave of holy irresistible pure Heavenly love! At once, Carol rose to her feet with arms high in the air, praising God as others around her were openly praising God, having been touched by His presence! The power of the Holy Spirit was incredibly strong that day and moving in the midst of the worshipers! His awesome presence was undisputable and undeniable!

While Carol was worshiping, the power of God supernaturally enabled her to see into the spirit world very clearly and vividly. She turned her head looking toward the left, and a few feet away she saw an incredibly brilliant white shimmering light! It was brighter than any light she had ever seen before on earth! It was like the sun with its rays pulsating outward!

In the center of the light, there stood Jesus, in all of His glorious beauty and exquisite radiance! It was impossible to tell if Jesus was a part of the light or if the light was a part of Him! Then Jesus extended His loving arms toward Carol!

Jesus spoke directly to Carol, saying, "I have healed you"! Carol was overcome with love and appreciation for His unbelievable revelation, although she silently thought to herself, "All of this for a case of indigestion?"

The following day Carol drove to a medical facility for a routine physical examination. When she told the doctor about the persistent indigestion, a nurse scheduled a "CT scan" straightaway for Carol. A "CT scan" (Computerized tomography), also known as a CAT scan (Computerized axial tomography) uses a computer that takes data from several X-ray images of structures inside a body and converts them into pictures on a monitor.

Carol was shocked when she learned the results of that procedure a couple of days later! The radiologist discovered a very large soft tissue mass, the size of a cantaloupe! Two Ultra Sounds, (specific diagnostic studies), confirmed the diagnosis. Carol saw a surgeon and he operated on her that Wednesday. The cooperative patient came through the surgical procedure and the removal of the mass satisfactorily. Then there came the waiting game! Biopsies had to be examined, and in two weeks Carol would learn if the mass was benign or malignant.

Those two weeks were stressful and would have been excruciatingly difficult, had it not been for the marvelous supernatural vision and holy message God provided for Carol on the previous Sunday! Carol realized why God had revealed Himself ahead of time. It was so that she could cling to the experience in hope, and by faith believing that God had already healed her! The biopsy result would confirm it! Perhaps the mass was cancerous before the holy manifestation. No matter what it was or wasn't, Jesus certainly rendered it harmless by His magnificent power! Otherwise He would not have told Carol, "I have healed you"!

But for you who revere My Name, the sun of righteousness will rise with healing in its rays (Malachi 4:2 NIV).

The vision was the weapon and the ammunition Carol used to win the battle with Satan when he came trying to put doubts in her mind, telling her she would surely die. When the two weeks had passed, Carol's doctor called her with the fantastic news! The report proved the mass was benign. Carol was officially healed in the natural world as well as the spiritual world! She could only thank the Lord and sing His praises by singing "Tis So Sweet to Trust in Jesus." Once again, the Lord showed up at just the right time!

Therefore let us draw near with confidence to the throne of grace, that we may receive mercy and may find grace to help in time of need (Hebrews 4:16).

Chapter 26

When God Healed the Deer

As the deer pants for the water brooks, so my soul pants for You, O God. (Psalm 42:1).

Christine Carter[10] and her husband lived on a small farm in middle Tennessee and wildlife roamed freely on their property. They were not hunters, but some of their neighbors were hunters who hunted and killed the deer in season. The woman cringed each time she heard gunshots, knowing that meant another beautiful deer had just lost its life.

It was early Monday morning when Christine found herself alone at home washing clothes and cleaning the house. Soon enough, she carried a basket of clean wet bed sheets outside to hang them on the line to dry. Half way through hanging the sheets on the line, Christine became aware that someone was watching her. It was the strangest feeling. She saw no one and she did not hear anything unusual. In her spirit, she sensed it strongly! Slowly, the woman turned around looking in all directions and towards the wooded area in back of the house. Then she spotted him!

There stood a full grown male deer with great antlers, standing silently beneath a large white dogwood tree! The woman and the deer made eye contact, but she remained as quiet as the deer! Very slowly the animal hobbled out into the open field, never taking his eyes off of her. Instantly Christine knew one of the hunters had injured him and she was so happy they did not succeed in killing the

10

lovely creature! She took a few steps toward the deer, then he took a few limping steps closer. She realized he was seriously injured or he would not be acting that way. He was desperately asking for help in the only way he knew how.

Christine knew better than to get too close. An injured deer with antlers and sharp hooves could easily kill a person. The two just stood there looking at each other. They were developing a sense of trust as they gazed at each other! She understood the Lord was calling upon her to pray for the animal. It was not her first time to hear God's voice or recognize His ways. She almost cried from sadness as she began to pray earnestly and sincerely for the wounded buck. After about five minutes the deer limped back into the woods.

The next morning Christine went out into the yard looking for the deer, and there he was patiently waiting for her. Just the same as the day before, the human and the animal tested each other and cautiously held their positions. She could feel the gaze of the deer's eyes searching her, looking for compassion and mercy. It was uncanny and unlike any previous encounter with any animal. Christine felt the Lord prompting her to pray once again and she did so willingly. After the prayer, the deer hobbled along finding his way back into seclusion and safety from human eyes.

For three weeks, Christine and the deer kept up the daily vigil. By the third week the deer was hobbling less and walking stronger than in earlier days. On the very last day she saw him, that marvelous creation, majestically prancing out of the woods with his head held high in the air! He had a regal air about him. At first he moved slowly without a sign of a slight limp. He stood there looking at her very still for about a minute before he bounded across the field taking broad leaps for the entire width of the property. He stopped only once and looked back as if to thank her, then he gracefully leapt over the barbed wire fence and vanished from sight!

Christine felt such a sense of relief for the deer! She never told anyone about the experience because the story would have seemed insignificant to one who did not see what happened with their own eyes! She offered up a prayer of thanksgiving to God for surely healing that animal, knowing God had called on her, requiring her faith to effectively complete the healing process.

As human beings we often don't understand why God wants, needs and requires us to pray and have faith in regards to what we are praying for, but that is the case. Certainly He has the power and the means to accomplish any matter that He chooses, but He wants our participation as "our part" in the marvelous blood Covenant that He has made with us. When we are obedient "in the natural," we move Him to activate His part, which is "supernatural." In a Covenant relationship, the weak party (us) can receive the strength of the stronger party (God). What an amazingly fantastic arrangement!

> *For My strength is made perfect in weakness* (2 Corinthians 12:9 KJV).

Christine Carter felt very special to have been called on to pray and to have been a part of such a spectacular healing miracle! One day, we will understand fully those things that we do not understand now. As Christians, we have so much to look forward to when we reach Heaven!

> *For now we see through a glass, darkly; but then face to face: now I know in part; but then shall I know even as also I am known* (1 Corinthians 13:12 KJV).

Chapter 27

The Voice of an Angel

Are they not all ministering spirits sent out to serve for the sake of those who are to inherit Salvation? (Hebrews 1:14).

Marla McDermott's mother-in-law, Debra, had battled liver cancer for 6 long years, so it came as no surprise when they learned that Hospice would be involved in her care beginning the next week. While it was not surprising, the news was sad and it was a sobering reminder that Debra's mortal life was about to end in a very short time, meaning a matter of weeks. Marla and her husband involved themselves in Debra's life as much as possible. However, Tennessee was a long way from Indianapolis, Indiana. The miles separated them and limited what they could do to really make a difference.

Marla was very troubled about Debra and the absence of a personal relationship with God in her life. Leaving this life is a frightening prospect for one who does not know Jesus! After all, there are only two final destinations available: Heaven and hell. Marla spent a lot of her time praying and reading her Bible and it gave her much needed peace for living her life. She sensed the Lord was prompting her to have a discussion with Debra about the condition of her soul.

The right time came sooner than Marla expected and she seized the opportunity. Marla shared all she knew about Jesus with Debra. She explained about repentance, forgiveness, and Salvation. Debra was extremely receptive to the idea and knowing she was at the end of her life, she prayed with Marla and asked Jesus to come into her heart; she was saved! She had no way of knowing it that day but she had less than 10 days to live!

> *Seek the LORD while He may be found. Call upon Him while He is near* (Isaiah 55:6).

It was very early in the morning on June 30, 2012 when Marla awoke to hear the voice of a woman, a soprano, singing softly just outside her window. She was very curious about the matter because this was "a first." She had never been awakened by someone serenading her! She looked everywhere, but found no one outside, so the voice remained a mystery.

Debra died peacefully later that same day, in the early evening. Marla was greatly comforted knowing that Debra died "saved" and confident that she was going to Heaven as her final eternal destination!

> *For God so loved the world, that He gave His only begotten Son, that WHOSOEVER believeth in Him should not perish, but have everlasting life* (John 3:16 KJV).

> *I most certainly understand now that God is not one to show partiality* (Acts 10:34).

> *People look at the outward appearance, but the LORD looks at the heart* (1 Samuel 16:7 NIV).

During the next few days, during the funeral proceedings, that knowledge gave family members great consolation, knowing about Debra's decision to be saved! Marla thought of the soprano voice more than once because the singing was angelic, unique, and even strange to some extent. The voice and the song sounded lovely but at the same time, it sounded other-worldly.

One week later, the same angelic soprano voice awakened Marla early in the morning! The voice originated from a spot just outside her bedroom window, but the one singing the song could not be seen by natural eyes. This time when the singing began, Marla just smiled and enjoyed the Heavenly music, knowing full well that no human voice was presenting the music. If an angel came to sing for their family, then Marla believed they should just be appreciative and take pleasure in the extraordinary gift! Their family received the performance as a sacred sign that all was well with Debra's soul!

Sing to the LORD, all the earth; proclaim good tidings of His Salvation from day to day (1 Chronicles 16:23).

Chapter 28

The Grip of Death

Do you not know that when you present yourselves to someone as slaves for obedience, you are slaves of the one whom you obey, either of sin resulting in death or of obedience resulting in righteousness? (Romans 6:16).

Terrell Lee[11] and his wife had two small children at a time when he worked in another state many days of the week. It was a very stressful time because the work, travel, and lack of communication actually created a hostile environment at home. The children suffered from missing their dad, and their mom tried to make everything better, but she was limited. She was a good mom, but she simply could not fill their dad's shoes because she was only one person.

There seemed to be little time for seeking God in those days, and Terrell found himself actually running from God in rebellion. Many times, he sensed in his spirit that God was convicting his heart and trying to draw him near to Himself. Each time, he resisted. At the time, Terrell thought he was self-sufficient and believed his sin was not as bad as the sins of others. Wrongly, he believed God would make an exception with him if he died, saying He would be happy to just overlook those sins. He thought to himself, "Surely a good God would not really send anyone to hell would He?" Actually, each one of us chooses where we will spend eternity by our own actions and choices. Terrell was deceived in his suppositions, as many people are at some point in their lives.

11

Terrell came home one weekend and he arrived at his house very late that night. When he entered the master bedroom he discovered his wife was asleep and their two small children were sleeping soundly on either side of their mom. It would be wiser to go and sleep in his son's bed than to wake them. Quietly, he left the room making his way down the hall in semi-darkness.

As Terrell entered the smaller bedroom, he was immediately aware that something was wrong. When he stepped through the doorway, it was like he just entered a different place and time. The temperature in the room was very different from the rest of the climate-controlled house. The little room was absolutely frigidly cold! He turned on the light and he could actually see his breath as he exhaled. The room was a fearful place, but he was too exhausted to worry about it at the time. The weary man proceeded by turning out the light and getting into bed as quickly as possible, hoping the warm covers would make him more comfortable.

While lying still in bed and forcing himself to relax, Terrell suddenly became terrified! He felt something moving close to the back of his neck, and in that moment a powerful hand came up through the mattress and grabbed him by the throat! With a death grip, the strong hand began forcefully pulling him downward, trying to pull him through the mattress! There was an evil presence hovering around the bed and just above his body! Terrell had no strength to resist, and he realized the powerful and dreaded entity was trying to kill him; it was choking him to death! Instantly he realized the thing was wretched and evil; it was not of this world! He believed it was a large demon or perhaps Satan himself!

Unable to move or speak, Terrell began silently praying for help, then mentally saying, "thinking" the name "Jesus" repeatedly! In rapid response to him mentally "speaking" that most powerful name above all names, "Jesus," the evil entity let go of his throat and his body moved back into place above the mattress as it was previously positioned.

> *That at the Name of Jesus, every knee should bow, of things in Heaven, and things in earth, and things under the earth* (Philippians 2:10 KJV).

Needless to say, in the days that followed, Terrell wasted no more time resisting God's intervention in his life. He discovered his Bible was meant for daily reading, being the spiritual food absolutely essential for his spirit within to grow. He now realized that his Bible was his only infallible travel guide for mortal and eternal life!

> *Simon Peter answered Him, "Lord, to whom shall we go? You have words of eternal life"* (John 6:68).

Soon after that horrible incident, Terrell experienced repentance, forgiveness and Salvation! The closeness of God never felt so right after having such an unimaginable and terrifying experience!

> *You are near, O LORD, and all Your commandments are truth* (Psalm 119:151).

Chapter 29

Help Me, Lord!

He will call upon Me, and I will answer him; I will be with him in trouble; I will rescue him and honor him (Psalm 91:15).

One day, Carol Brown left her home in Orlando, Florida to run some errands and her first stop was the post office. When she returned to her car she used the remote to unlock the door, got in, and closed the door. For no apparent reason, the alarm shrieked so loudly that Carol could hardly think straight! She frantically surveyed the dashboard, searching for a button to press that might turn the alarm off, but she saw no such device! The noise continued and Carol had no idea what to do except to drive home. She was certain that her husband, Ed, would know how to shut it off!

Carol started the car and drove onto the street where the car promptly stalled and the motor died. The car would not budge an inch! The key was, by design, locked in the ignition and the car door was locked as well! The safety feature was thorough! It would have been great if a thief was making his getaway in the car, but that was not the case!

The innocent car owner was at that moment trapped inside with no way out. Carol attempted to use her cell phone to call her husband, but the phone was also rendered useless! Stranded there in the middle of a busy street with drivers honking their horns and telling her to move her car out of the way, Carol noticed a man walking on the sidewalk. She called out to the man asking if she could use his cell phone. He allowed Carol to use his phone. Her husband did not recognize the strange number of the incoming call, therefore, he did not answer it.

On the verge of panic, Carol finally thought to herself, "Well I guess the only thing left to do now is to pray!" Immediately, Carol was a little disappointed that she had not prayed first thing! In the past, Carol had heard others make that same statement in reference to their own circumstances and it had always bothered her that humans put off until last the most important action of praying that should be carried out first! Carol did not delay, and at that very moment she prayed a powerful and to-the-point prayer crying, "Help me, Lord!"

At once, the Most High God saw fit to turn off the alarm and turn on all the gadgets that were previously locked by the security system. When Carol attempted to start the car, the key freely turned and the engine started as normally as ever. Carol laughed out loud and thanked her Heavenly Father! She knew God had caused her to experience a small crisis and His deliverance as a lesson and reminder of His amazing Grace! Driving home, she realized she was making a joyful noise unto the Lord as she sang His praises all the way!

Shout joyfully to the LORD, all the earth; break forth and sing for joy and sing praises (Psalm 98:4).

Chapter 30

The Apparition on Orchard Road

*Now He was telling them a parable to show that at all
times they ought to pray and not lose heart* (Luke 18:1).

Mary Kahle of Millville, New Jersey was a single woman, living
alone and on her own in 2007, working as an independent care giver.
When her sister Harriet, recently widowed, moved from her home
state of North Carolina to Millville, Mary invited her to come and
live with her. The arrangement was a wise financial move and it
suited the two sisters, who truly enjoyed spending time together.

Time passed quickly and two years later in 2009, Mary became
the proud grandmother of an adorable little girl whose name was
Jenna. When Jenna was 7 weeks old, Harriet agreed to begin caring
for the infant while her parents worked, beginning on the following
Monday morning. On that Friday evening prior to the much
anticipated Monday morning when Harriet would assume her new
responsibilities as Jenna's baby sitter, Mary and Harriet stayed up
until nearly midnight, laughing and talking as joyfully as two young
school girls!

At the end of the evening, they each headed for their own bedroom,
but not before saying "good night"! Mary said to Harriet, "Good
night Sissy, I love you." Harriet responded to Mary by echoing those
very same words! It was a ritual they each treasured, for saying those
words to each other always caused them to remember their wonderful
childhood and growing up with loving parents who cherished them.
Those were the last words spoken that night. Unfortunately, it was

the last opportunity either of them would ever have to say "good night" to one another in their earthly lifetimes.

Around 6:30 the next morning, Mary awoke to the sound of Harriet's small dog, Jordan, whining and crying for someone to let him go outside. Mary wondered why "Sissy" had not already done so. Usually, Harriet let Jordan out way before six o'clock; but not that morning. Mary walked into the kitchen and that is when she discovered Harriet lying on the floor, dead. She had died of a sudden and unexpected heart attack, silently falling there on the kitchen floor where she remained until Mary found her that Saturday morning. Mary was devastated by the sudden and unexpected separation from her dearly loved sister. Harriet's children made arrangements for Harriet's body to be returned to North Carolina for burial next to her husband.

It was two weeks after Harriet passed away and Mary was leaving the home of one of her clients to go to the home of another client. Mary was finding it tremendously difficult to cope with her loss. She and Harriet were close. However, she had never realized just how deeply she cared for her sister. The forlorn sister questioned the Lord, asking Him why He took her sister, knowing full well how much they needed each other. She was only 62 at the time of her death and that seemed very young, considering she might have lived another twenty-five or thirty years! Mary was driving along normally on Orchard Road in Vineland, New Jersey when she found herself sobbing. She felt as if her heart was about to break.

Looking straight ahead and continuing to drive in spite of her tears, Mary was shocked speechless when she clearly saw a figure, appearing to be Jesus, suspended in mid-air just ahead of her! His body was about 5 feet above the pavement and His arms were extended and open forming a semi-circle like He was offering her

His consolation! It was not at all like she was going to hit Him with the car. As she drove forward, the Jesus-looking figure remained the same distance from her car as if the car and His presence were in a time capsule, traveling in unison in a very controlled environment. "Jesus" was wearing an all-white robe and all other colors were nonexistent based on what Mary saw and mentally comprehended. She saw only pure glowing white light!

At the wonderful and incomprehensible sight of seeing the vision of the Lord Jesus, Mary's sobs became more prevalent, necessitating the need for her to pull her car over to the side of the road. When she came to a stop, the vison vanished. Never in her entire lifetime had Mary felt so emotionally moved by anything she had seen or experienced as the clearly visible vision of the Lord! It was extraordinary!

After several minutes, Mary pulled herself together, dried her tears and drove on to the home of her next client. She completed her work that afternoon even though she was shaken to the core of her being. When she arrived at her home later that day, she was aware that she was abnormally tired, absolutely exhausted, and in need of sound sleep.

Earlier than usual, Mary turned off all the lights to achieve total darkness in her bedroom. Even a faint glow from a light usually kept her awake. As long as she could remember, she had needed a very dark room for sleeping. Lying there in the darkness, talking quietly with the Lord, she asked Him, "Can it really be that I saw Your face, Lord?" Mary questioned the vision she saw earlier on Orchard Road.

Suddenly, Mary was shocked for the second time in a matter of hours! The distinguishable face of one believed to be Jesus appeared out of the darkness and she could clearly see His magnificent eyes! She was entranced! They were unlike any eyes she could remember. Bluish green eyes filled with a certain love and undeniable compassion, adorned His face. Loosely curled shoulder length brown hair rimmed the face of the One she supposed to be the Lord. The Lord then spoke to Mary, saying, "Move on"! Heaven was reassuring her that she had indeed been the recipient of a rare and holy manifestation! Furthermore, she accepted the message, meaning she should move ahead, not looking back or longing for what might have been. She knew she was to focus on God alone!

> *Set your mind on things above, not on the things below*
> (Colossians 3:2).

The moment the lovely face faded away, there in the darkness Mary watched a small white cloud materialize. There was shining white light behind the little cloud that strangely appeared. Then it changed into a white dove! Quickly the dove spread its wings and flew into the darkness and out of sight. Immediately the process happened again from start to finish until the white dove flew away. That incident happened four times before the supernatural activity ceased to be on that memorable night! Moments later, Mary entered a very deep and restful sleep! She had heard of counting sheep to encourage sleep but never had she heard of counting white doves! Never the less, it worked quite well.

When she awoke the next morning, Mary felt rested and rejuvenated, and the loneliness oddly seemed distant. The reality that she was alone in life was still present. However, she had a new awareness that Jesus was with her every minute and every hour! She was totally mindful of the fact that she would never truly be alone again. During that deep slumber, God must have imparted a certain consciousness into her spirit, reminding her that He would surely be with her unto the very end!

The Scripture that came alive in her heart that morning was the one that gives her an uncommon sense of peace even now. This is the Scripture that keeps her mind at ease:

> *And the peace of God, which surpasses all comprehension, will guard your hearts and your minds in Christ Jesus* (Philippians 4:7).

Chapter 31

The Connector

Draw near to God and he will draw near to you (James 4:8).

Janna Landers[12] often walked the long, narrow, winding road that led from a side door of the farmhouse to the old barn situated on the back of their property. She and her husband, Luke, had owned the Tennessee farm only three years, but sometimes she felt like she had lived there most of her life. As she walked the gravel road to the barn, praying, a sweet sense of peace covered her like an invisible Heavenly dome.

Janna lived most of her life separate from God, as most humans do before God's reveals Himself in undeniable ways, allowing the person the opportunity to receive Him or reject Him. At the age of 39, Janna was eager to accept Jesus, turning away from worldly ways to the simple life she now shared with her husband Luke.

The woman had heard many stories about how God revealed Himself to those who were seeking Him and she found herself searching everywhere for evidence of God's presence! On that cold late winter day, Janna was helping Luke search for a small metal connector, a mechanical part for the tractor and trailer. It must have fallen out of his pocket somewhere between the house and the barn as he drove the small John Deere tractor to store it inside the barn. Luke said it was a lost cause. Finding that two inch silver connector in the silver-white limestone gravel would be like finding a needle

---

12

in a hay stack! He told Janna He would order a replacement. Still, Janna saw an opportunity in their misfortune!

Slowly and deliberately, Janna walked, taking one careful step at a time, her eyes scanning the small pieces of rock. She prayed one of her ordinary simple prayers saying, "Lord, please help me find that connector. Just let my eyes rest upon it and I will know it is Your doing."

While the temperature was surely cold, around 38 degrees, the blue sky and warm sunshine resting on her back made the day seem a lot warmer than it was. Janna smiled, still in awe of how real God made Himself to her in their relatively new relationship between a Heavenly Father and His child.

After five minutes of walking, praying and looking, Janna glanced ahead, a short distance farther down the road. To her astonishment, she saw a slender ray of brilliant white glowing light from above radiating to one particular spot on the road! It was maybe ten feet ahead of where she was standing. Suddenly, a silver sparkle radiated toward her from where the brilliant ray of light landed on the road! Janna smiled, beaming inside, knowing God was showing her the connector she was praying to find!

Running ahead, Janna reached her hand down toward the silver shimmer of light! With her thumb and fore finger, she picked up the tiny "lost and found" connector for which she had been searching! The holy ray of light vanished as she retrieved the lost object, but not before she acknowledged her prayer had been answered by the Most High God!

Janna ran the rest of the way to the barn, laughing and praising the Lord for showing up and revealing Himself to her in a simple manifestation on that beautiful winter day! Luke believed Janna's story, but he did not fully share her enthusiasm. His eyes had not witnessed the beam of light sent from Heaven! Those special intimate moments that occur in everyday life may seem small to the rest of the world, but to the mind behind the eyes of the one watching God evidence Himself, it is no small thing! It is a miracle!

For God, who commanded the light to shine out of darkness, hath shined in our hearts, to give the light of the knowledge of the glory of God in the face of Jesus Christ (2 Corinthians 4:6).

Chapter 32

Lord, Show Me

But seek ye first the Kingdom of God, and His righteousness; and all these things shall be added unto you (Matthew 6:33 KJV).

Lindy Hooper[13] was a woman that placed a high priority on seeking the Lord first in her daily decisions, large and small. She spent much time daily, feeding her spirit with the daily bread of the Word of God! Therefore, it was very natural for her to stop, pray, and then wait for an answer from the Lord before acting. Her reasoning for seeking God's direction first followed along these lines: If we really and truly believe God is real, that He is involved in every hour of our lives, that He wants what is best for us; why do we not stop and pray every single time before taking an action that might result in an outcome that is less than acceptable?

Not long ago, there had been a situation in which she was involved and quite honestly in which she had been deliberately humiliated more than once. She made up her mind to speak in truth and honesty, then withdraw from the situation, refusing to be drawn into it again in the future. The conversation had to take place by telephone or e-mail, since distance was a significant factor. Lindy preferred a verbal conversation in lieu of an e-mail. Her temper was cool, but she had had enough and she was certain this would be alright with God.

13

Thankfully, she stopped long enough to pray before picking up the telephone and making the call.

Set a guard, O LORD, over my mouth; keep watch over the door of my lips (Psalm 141:3).

She asked the Lord to help her, telling Him she wanted to do whatever pleased Him. She said, "If I am wrong please stop me, and keep this call from happening." She prayed at 15 minutes past 9:00 a.m., planning to make the call at 9:30 a.m. She waited patiently, allowing God 15 minutes in which He could answer her.

At 9:25 a.m., Lindy lifted the phone receiver, looking up as if looking into the Lord's face and said, "Okay Lord, let's see if the phone still works! That's one way You could stop me. You could shut the phone service down." Then she laughed. Lindy placed the receiver to her ear and discovered there was only silence, no dial tone! With raised eyebrows, she held the receiver away from her face, looking into the earpiece as if she could see what was wrong. She walked across the room to her desk and discovered the computer had no internet service. Then, using her cell phone, the dumbfounded woman called the carrier, and the prompts led her to a recording advising they were having technical difficulty in her area.

At 9:35 a.m. she approached the phone and picked up the receiver with a great deal of reverence in her demeanor. She was not laughing. In seconds, she realized the Lord had surely answered the prayer she prayed earlier, because this time she clearly heard a normal dial tone!

God did not want her to make that call, so He shut down the phone and computer service for 10 minutes. It was as simple as that. Needless to say, Lindy, by her own admission, did some more praying, but with more humility this time. The incident was a definite reminder that God is watching and listening to all we do and say!

> *The LORD looks from Heaven, He sees all the sons of men* (Psalm 33:13).

Looking back on it all, she was amazed that someone as awesome and magnificent as Almighty God intervenes in our ordinary and sometimes seemingly insignificant circumstances. Certainly He delegates authority, and realistically she suspected it was her angel that manipulated the phone service that morning. Still she knew that all divine intervention is directly from God, caused by His will. God knows all, sees all, and instructs the angels!

> *Bless the LORD, ye His angels, that excel in strength, that do His commandments, hearkening unto the voice of His Word* (Psalm 103:20 KJV).

Lindy had seen things such as the present day incident happen more than once. She knew that God was involved in even the smallest details of our lives! She thought: if God is involved with the small things, consider how much more He is involved with greater and more important matters in our lives!

We should all be reminded of His power and His ability to work for us and in our favor. If we have sought HIM "first," then we will often see miraculous guidance in matters that are too complex for us to handle! Truly the "battle," or "supernatural part" is not ours, but God's, and surely He will perform it when we have done our part "in the natural"!

Thus saith the LORD unto you, be not afraid nor dismayed by reason of this great multitude; FOR THE BATTLE IS NOT YOURS, BUT GOD'S (2 Chronicles 20:15 KJV).

Chapter 33

Happy Birthday!

Every good thing given and every perfect gift is from above, coming down from the Father of lights, with whom there is no variation or shifting shadow (James 1:17).

In 2012, Carol Brown celebrated her 80th birthday! Carol's oldest son, John, and his wife, Eileen, drove Carol and her husband, Ed, to see her youngest son, Alan, for the day. Alan is the Food and Beverage Director for a lovely hotel right on Daytona Beach in Florida. Other family members were invited to take part in the celebration. Carol was pleasantly surprised and enormously pleased to see and spend time with those she loved on her special day!

The family spent a magnificent day together! When the day was nearly over, the family drove home with Carol and Ed happily sitting together in the back seat of the car. Carol was silently giving thanks to the Lord for all the love and good wishes she had received that day! Suddenly, a thought just popped into her mind and the thought was, "Lord, I have had so many Happy Birthday wishes today; I just wish I could hear from You!"

Carol was thinking that might be an unusual wish, but she could not refrain from thinking it. As if on cue, Carol looked out the window to her right, and there in the distance, against a dark night sky she saw a very large green neon sign displaying the words, "HAPPY BIRTHDAY"!

The sign was very much alone. There were no buildings, hotels or restaurants nearby, just the sign! Carol was flabbergasted and amazed that He answered her so quickly and so undeniably! "Thank You Lord," echoed in Carol's heart!

God must enjoy interacting with His children. We cannot imagine how much enjoyment the angels get when they are called upon to carry out God's instructions. It makes us wonder if the green neon sign was still there the next day, or if God simply spoke it into temporary existence at a moment's notice! He is able! Carol's 80th birthday was made memorable by many people and many actions, but God's birthday greeting stood high above all the rest, literally!

Delight yourself in the Lord and He will give you the desires of your heart (Psalm 37:4).

Chapter 34

A Patch of Blue

Thus says the LORD, your Redeemer, the Holy One of Israel, "I am the LORD your God, who teaches you to profit, Who leads you in the way you should go" (Isaiah 48:17).

Lynette Gettis[14] arrived in the office of her Optometrist, Dr. Hammond, just minutes before her appointment. She was due for an annual examination even though she was not experiencing any abnormal symptoms. She liked going to that particular office because the doctor was an old friend. The two rarely saw each other because their worlds carried them in different directions, but each of them enjoyed the yearly get together! They were able to share the latest news on their families and what was happening in their lives.

The "doc" finished his exam and surprised Lynette by announcing he would like to dilate her eyes and take a more in-depth look at her eyes, if she didn't mind. Of course she didn't mind. However, she was somewhat hesitant because of the way the procedure would affect her vision. Lynette knew she would not be able to see anything up close. She would not be able to dial a phone or see the speedometer on her car. Her overall vision would be compromised for several hours. Still, she agreed and the doctor completed the dilation and exam.

Lynette left the doctor's office wearing sunglasses to protect her eyes from the light. Her pupils were fully dilated and focusing was

_____

14

troublesome. She proceeded confidently that morning, being certain that she would manage the 10 mile drive home. Lynette planned to move cautiously and slowly. She would stay in the far right lane and meander along until she reached the secondary road leading to her neighborhood.

Driving proved to be tricky. Lynette squinted her eyes to keep as much of the light out as possible, but she had to leave her eyes open enough to see where she was going. Silently she prayed, asking God to help her travel carefully and to guide her safely home in His own way.

It was at that moment when Lynette saw a patch of blue ahead of her. She kept her eyes focused on that large patch of blue and drove in a straight line, no longer having to watch for the lines painted on the road. What a blessing! The miles clicked over on her odometer and in a short time, Lynette found herself at her familiar intersection where she turned onto the road that would carry her home. The patch of blue continued on in another direction at that point.

She arrived home safely and the drive was uneventful, but for the rest of the day, Lynette thought of that patch of blue! In reality the patch of blue was a very large blue tarpaulin draped over someone's cargo on a towing trailer hitched to a truck. If the words, "follow me" had been placed on the tailgate of the truck ahead of her, it would not have been more beneficial. The blue tarp size and color was precisely what Lynette's dilated eyes needed at that time! Without the tarp, the trip would have been possible, but very tedious!

Lynette never mentioned the incident to anyone because others might have thought it was just a coincidence. Lynette would have strongly disagreed! Too many times she had witnessed God's divine intervention and she recognized the circumstance for exactly what it was! God moved His loving hand of providence on her behalf, sending a truck and blue tarp in her direction. It was easy to see that large target. All she had to do was keep her eyes on the patch of blue all the way home!

Lynette smiled many times during the day over that sweet and seemingly insignificant incident. God is always watching and listening to His children and He is so willing to answer when we ask with expectant faith! Perhaps we should ask more often, then watch for His holy answers to manifest. All things really are possible with God!

Jesus looked at them and said, "With man this is impossible, but with God all things are possible" (Matthew 19:26).

Chapter 35

Healing Power and Saving Grace

The prayer offered in faith will restore the one who is sick and the Lord will raise him up and if he has committed any sins, they will be forgiven him, (James 5:15).

John White seriously injured his back one day while working at a dairy farm. He was sharing a home with his elderly mother in Donna, Texas when the incident occurred. The pain became more severe with each passing day, progressing to the point where John became bed ridden. He rarely got out of bed and he required crutches to move the shortest distances. John was a strong man, yet tears welled up in his eyes at times from the excruciating pain that had become unbearable.

Members of his church visited him and prayed for John to be healed, but the prayers went unanswered while he grew worse with each passing day. Two weeks went by and John was admittedly in a desperate situation. His doctor would operate on him, but warned him that low back injuries were not always surgically correctable. With surgery John might get better, get worse, or stay the same. One chance out of three for getting better from an operation did not make a lot of sense to John. He still believed God could and would heal him.

Responding to John's request, one of his friends came by one morning, to drive him to the church. On crutches and with great difficulty, John managed to endure the ride and get out of the car upon arrival. He was in dire need of relief and believed it might help to go inside the church to pray for God to heal him. An evangelist from Greenville, South Carolina was holding a crusade at the church that week. The man had parked his camper next to the church and he happened to see John hobbling toward the building.

Once inside the sanctuary, John made his way to the front pew. John was in so much pain that he could not sit so he stretched out on the long bench for a few moments. The preacher from South Carolina entered the church and made his way to where John was lying down. He asked John if he would allow him to pray for him to be healed and John eagerly responded by a resounding "yes!"

The pastor proceeded by laying his hands on John's head while he prayed a simple audible prayer. Absolutely nothing happened until he finished praying and removed his hands from John's head. Suddenly, a ball of warm supernatural power, seemingly the size of a golf ball, entered the top of John's head then traveled slowly down to his neck and down through his spine. John did not know what was happening! It felt like hot liquid had been poured into his body! The warm ball of holy, healing power traveled slowly growing warmer and warmer until it reached the injured portion of John's back. In an instant John's pain vanished and so did the warm flowing power!

John sat up slowly then placed his feet on the floor. Carefully, he stood up and stretched in all directions. The pain was gone! John began taking long steps walking up and down the aisle proving that he was pain free! It was clearly obvious that John had been supernaturally healed from the top of his head to the soles of his feet!

John eagerly began praising and thanking the Lord for His miraculous gift of healing through the traveling evangelist! John found it was impossible to keep from smiling! The healed man picked up his crutches then walked briskly and normally to his friend's car!

And by His stripes we are healed (Isaiah 53:5 KJV).

John's mom was standing on the porch when they returned home, at which time he climbed out of the car and walked normally toward the house. His mom was amazed because she had been his caregiver for the previous two weeks. She was truly aware of the seriousness of his condition. She had carried his meals to him in bed and watched him cry in agony. When Mrs. White saw him walking normally and free from pain, she became aware of the fact that a healing miracle had actually occurred!

John told his mom every detail of how the preacher prayed for him just before God miraculously sent healing power into his body! John's mother was not a believer at the time, but after John's miracle she became very intrigued by the power and reality of the awesome God of Abraham, Isaac and Jacob! Mrs. White was able to get her hands on a Bible and she began reading it day after day until one day, a second miracle happened! The Scriptures came to life for Mrs. White and by God's incomprehensible power she understood the Gospel was true! She accepted Jesus as her Savior! She was saved and it became evident by her change of heart!

Neither John nor his mother would ever be the same again! Mrs. White was changed and her faith comforted her as the Word sustained her until the time of her death. She was 84 years old when she died.

John never experienced another back pain from the injury that had incapacitated him! After God healed John, he decided to go into full time mission work. He traveled to Mexico and remained there for several years before returning to Texas. And to think, it all began with suffering! Because of the suffering, lives were changed, a body was healed and at least one soul was saved!

Now unto Him that is able to do exceeding abundantly above all that we ask or think, according to the power that worketh in us (Ephesians 3:20 KJV).

Chapter 36

Visions to Show the Way

Call to Me, and I will answer you, and will tell you great and mighty things which you do not know (Jeremiah 33:3).

Elizabeth White was brought up in the Episcopalian Protestant Church. However, she never considered herself to be highly religious. She lived her life according to man's rules, not really knowing about God's laws. She and her husband, Herb, were living in Bourne, Massachusetts when Herb discovered he had lung cancer. Although he was dying of cancer, a heart attack abruptly ended his life on February 28, 2007. Herb was 69 years old when he died.

Before Elizabeth could fully adapt to the loss of her husband, her 44 year old son died of a heart attack just 7 months later. Those two deaths of loved ones brought about an enormous amount of grief and also many questions for Elizabeth. Her mind did not contain the answers to the deep questions that bombarded her thoughts daily. Slowly but surely, Elizabeth's spirit was drawn to the reality of God. A diligent search for His presence in the midst of the suffering, trials, and tribulations providentially began to reshape her life!

It was around that time that Elizabeth began experiencing some supernatural occurrences that she simply could not explain. Strange happenings took place at night while Elizabeth was in bed during the quiet hours while she was waiting for sleep to overtake her. The first incident involved a very small white angel. The little angel appeared in her bedroom for just a moment in midair, crossing right in front of her face, then quickly vanished from sight!

The second incident was when Elizabeth was awakened abruptly at which time she became aware of an unfamiliar man sitting in a chair beside her bed in the partially lit room. He wore a gray linen robe and he sat there very still with his face toward the door, intently watching, seemingly as a protector or a guardian angel watching over Elizabeth. When the man realized Elizabeth was looking directly at him, his appearance blurred, then he faded out of sight.

Other episodes followed, and if a message was associated with each appearance, Elizabeth was unable to determine what that might be. The night visions came often, and Elizabeth described her ability to see them as one seeing a hologram. A hologram is a three-dimensional image formed by the interference of light beams from a particular light source. Once she saw a beautiful brown Labrador retriever joyfully turning its head from side to side!

On one occasion Elizabeth saw the scene of an entire cemetery, the grave stones and shrubbery associated with the burial grounds. There were many unfamiliar people there, interacting with one another on an elevated stage, going up and down the stair case to one side of the stage. There was another time when she saw a dining room meal-time setting in which her deceased mother and father were present and seated at the table. The room setting resembled the dining room that belonged to her parents in earlier times.

Elizabeth had one vision of a pretty little blonde-haired girl wearing a sweet smile! She was very young and her face resembled Elizabeth's face as she recalled it from some of her own childhood photographs. At that very moment, her mind was drawn to a specific and painful life event. It was the miscarriage she suffered when she was a young woman. She felt certain that the little girl was her precious unborn daughter, although she could not be certain!

There were multiple visions of chickens, cows, sheep and various farm animals. Along with that scenery there was a slender woman dressed in a long dress and hair bonnet, strolling through a broad field of grass. She appeared to be feeding the animals. The woman's clothing definitely indicated she must have lived in a previous century! Repeatedly, she has seen a single blue eye watching her. Once she saw her deceased husband appear briefly and disappear after only a few seconds. There was a time when she saw a beautiful setting of a narrow gate standing before a lovely sunrise! She wondered if it was a gate leading to Heaven!

Other visions of similar nature entered the world of Elizabeth White, always showing up under the influence of quiet solitude and semi-darkness. She believed the visions were a spiritual gift from God to remind her of His presence in her life. It seemed like God was teaching her there was another world beside the present one, a spiritual world, as proclaimed by the Bible!

While the visions were vague by description, they served an important purpose! While she was the recipient of those ongoing visions, Elizabeth's curiosity about spiritual matters grew until she increased her search for God. It was during those seeking and searching days that Elizabeth expanded her search for answers to the Holy Bible! Elizabeth soon realized the Scriptures were alive and true! One Scripture was especially beneficial to her!

In humility receive the Word implanted which is able to save your soul (James 1:21).

In 2008, Elizabeth repented, asked God's forgiveness, and received Jesus as her Lord and Savior! By her own admission, it was the combination of losing her loved ones to death coupled with the visions that stirred her spirit and ultimately led her to become a Christian! God knows exactly what will speak to each of us and what it is that will affect our souls!

Chapter 37

Signs and Wonders

Once more He (Jesus Christ) visited Cana in Galilee, where He had turned the water into wine (John 4:46 NIV).

In 1976, God inspired Al Zappola, of Gibbstown, New Jersey to write a message pertaining to the Crucifixion and Resurrection of Jesus Christ and to make a Roman Centurion costume. (In ancient Rome, "centurion" referred to a captain of 100 foot soldiers. The centurion was loyal, courageous, and skilled in battle.) Al's costume consisted of even the details of the Centurion's spear, shield, sword and plumed helmet! The Lord did not reveal when or where He was to use them. Al also created sound effects for the whip that lashed the body of Jesus, the hammer striking the nails in His hands and feet, the noise of the crowds, the voice of Jesus as He spoke with his last breath, the reverberations of the trembling earth at His death and the excitement of the Resurrection in the "Hallelujah Chorus"!

That Easter, Al's Pastor became ill suddenly and called on Al to deliver the Easter message. Al was already prepared, for God had prepared him! He put on the Roman Centurion costume the Lord had directed him to make, and delivered the message that was given to him. It was an eyewitness account of Jesus Christ's last days of ministry on earth as well as His Resurrection.

Over the next ten years, Al gave his presentation to congregations wherever he was called upon to do so. During those years, several props were added. A six-foot tall cross, a purple robe, and a real woven crown of thorns were among them. When the end of the tenth year of the Centurion ministry was approaching, Al decided to add a pitcher and bowl as a visual image when he demonstrated Pilate washing his hands of the decision to crucify Jesus, placing the blame on those in the crowd, as recorded in the Holy Bible's account in Matthew 27:24.

That year Al was uncertain if he should continue his ministry since opportunities for sharing his presentation had decreased. Al and his wife, Sherry, entered a time of prayer, asking God to give them a sign if the presentation should continue.

The 10th anniversary arrived, and on the day of the scheduled Christian drama presentation, Al and Sherry presented "The Roman Centurion." The hand-washing segment went as planned. However, after the drama, they returned from having refreshments and were shocked to discover the water had turned red! They looked at each other and at the water. It was as if someone had really washed their bloody hands in it! They tried to explain it away. Al and Sherry thought maybe the vinyl armor, or the leather belt, on the hilt of the sword had bled when Al washed his hands.

They experimented, trying to duplicate the processes they thought might have caused the water to turn red, but they were not able to reproduce any color! When they examined the white towel used to wipe Al's hands, thinking there would be some color on; it was still very wet, but perfectly white.

There seemed to be no explanation. They actually imagined a "prankster" had poured some punch into the bowl while they were away, but the water was an entirely different color than the punch. They could not understand, but finally accepted that the water could only have turned blood-red by supernatural means.

To empty the water for cleanup, they decided to empty it into the pitcher for less chance of spillage. However, the Lord had a better plan! As they poured the water, it became perfectly clear right before their eyes! You can imagine their shock! That's right, clear!

The Lord spoke volumes to Al and Sherry that night, saying, "Now do you believe I changed it?" They were speechless. They actually thought no one would believe them, so they decided to just go home. However, on the way, they couldn't help but stop at the pastor's house and share their story with him, wanting to know his opinion.

The pastor said, "You prayed for a sign, why do you doubt God's answer? O ye of little faith!" Ever since that day of the supernatural incident, they began sharing the miraculous sign with each Centurion presentation. From that day forward, they never again questioned the reality of the sign God gave them in response to their prayer for a sign! God sent the sign, therefore, Al and Sherry committed to sharing the Roman Centurion presentation every time they were invited to perform!

Al still ministers with the Centurion, Barabbas, Judas and he recently added The High Priest. His latest message is on the three Temples, the last being the one that will be built in our own end times. In full costume Al presents charts and his handcrafted replica of the "Ark of the Covenant." He never develops a character unless the Lord compels him to do so.

Each time Al and Sherry do a presentation, they share their story of God's gift, the sign He gave them: The time He changed ordinary water into blood-stained water right before their eyes. Then He turned the blood-stained water into perfectly clear water as He evidenced His presence in a powerful and memorable way! Miracles do still happen if we only believe!

> *Truly, truly, I (Jesus Christ) say to you, he who believes in Me, the works that I do, he will do also; and greater works than these he will do; because I go to the Father* (John 14:12).

Chapter 38

Killy Kranky Laury

It will also come to pass that before they call, I will answer; and while they are still speaking, I will hear (Isaiah 65:24).

Killy Kranky Laury was a small Yorkshire Terrier belonging to one Charles Laury of Millville, New Jersey! A dog with a sweeter and more playful disposition could not be found anywhere! Charles enjoyed caring for the happy dog and when a friend brought him a new collar for the pup, Charles eagerly placed the handsome collar around his furry neck. The trouble came when he took Killy for his first walk wearing the collar that was then attached to the leash. A faulty snap caused the collar to come undone and that was a "game changer"! As soon as Killy realized he was as free as a bird, he made a mad dash down the street!

Charles began chasing Killy down Oakwood Drive, then around and around a neighbor's home. The out- of-control dog then crossed the street in the midst of oncoming traffic with Charles in pursuit! Charles was panting and out of breath by that time. However, the animal was just getting started! Killy thought it was a wonderful game, apparently thinking he had never seen his master as playful and energetic as he was that day! That knowledge encouraged the dog and he continued to run the entire length of Oakwood Street a second time. He turned and ran past Holy Cross Cemetery, looking back toward Charles every now and then. The dog was more than likely checking to see if Charles was still in the game! Charles was keeping up as well as he could considering the fact that his heart was pounding and perspiration was trickling down his face like streams of tears!

The frolicking dog then headed for one of the busier streets past the neighborhood, and that was when and where Charles stopped, knowing he was "done for"! He could not run another ten seconds! He stood there trying to catch his breath, watching that wild dog run, when it dawned on him that he really needed to ask God for some help!

Charles spoke out loud as he prayed, saying, "Lord I need some help! I just can't go any farther!" At that very instant two pickup trucks came to a sudden stop. The trucks were heading in opposite directions, but the drivers both stopped on cue as if God had shouted a command to them! Both men then raised their arms high above their heads as if working in unison! Suddenly, the dog stopped and all four legs just folded beneath him. He did not move another inch! That is how God answered Charles's prayer!

The answer to the prayer came so quickly! It was apparent that the actions taken by those two men were done out of obedience to a discernible holy voice that commanded them to help Charles Laury!

Charles said it was one of the most beautiful and incredible things to watch that he had ever witnessed! The moment the prayer was prayed, God sent the answer! It was like counting, "one, two, and three"!

Charles has recalled this answered prayer to mind on many occasions when he has prayed, needing timely help, and he has shared the story on many occasions with others. Charles said, "When you have a need, all you have to do is ask God. He doesn't answer all prayers, but in His knowledge and wise judgment, He knows which prayers to answer and when to answer them. He is an excellent God and I am so glad I have Him over my life!"

> *But my God shall supply all your need according to His riches in glory by Christ Jesus.* (Philippians 4:19 KJV).

Chapter 39

Suffering is a Supernatural Experience

And we know that God causes all things to work together for good to those who love God, to those who are called according to His purpose (Romans 8:28).

When Kyle Bates was 19 years old, the Lord sent him a vision, revealing he would one day share his life's story in order to help mankind. Kyle was very serious when he discussed the details of his story with me, believing that in doing so, he had fulfilled the portion of his obligation. He entrusted to me the task of shedding light on his life experiences in such a way as to enable readers to benefit from reading it. Kyle's story begins with the next paragraph.

No doubt about it, Kyle had been through a lot in 40+ years, but what did it all mean? He had asked himself the same question many times. After prayerfully considering all the facts, this belief emerged: perhaps his lifetime of challenges might be an illustration of how God often- times works in the hearts, minds, and lives of His children. If we will only trust Him through the good and the bad times, at a time of God's own choosing, He will one day provide us with a really good explanation for everything that we have endured. It helps us to remember that miracles come in various shapes and sizes; and if God gives out a million miracles in one day, each gift bag will be different and unique! Sometimes we fail to recognize a miracle when we see one, especially if the miracle is made up of pain, tears or suffering!

Kyle's earliest memories of growing up in Southern California until he reached the fifth grade were pleasant remembrances! He was happy about everything and he had reason to be happy! It was customary for neighboring children to come together on his street and at his home where games, laughter, and good times were a way of life. . Those kids were friends he had grown up with and Kyle was a happy child without a worry in the world! Kyle was a handsome boy with a year-round tan! His smile came naturally, and people were attracted to him because of his good looks, quick wit, and that ever present charismatic grin! Once he was even awarded the title of "King of Smiles" in a school contest. It was a fitting title!

Most of the time, Kyle felt special and he liked it, particularly being popular and getting far more attention than anyone else. He was developing an attitude of arrogance, although he did not see it as harmful. A strange power had subtly entered Kyle's mind and thought processes. He could not define the influence, but neither could he deny it. Many years passed before Kyle was able to accurately characterize the intruder as pride.

> *For all that is in the world, the lust of the flesh, and the lust of the eyes, and the pride of life, is not of the Father, but is of the world* (I John 2:16).

> *In whom the god of this world hath blinded the minds of them which believe not, lest the light of the glorious gospel of Christ, who is the image of God, should shine unto them* (2 Corinthians 4:4 KJV).

Over the next four years, Kyle's father received promotions that took him from being a foreman over a handful of people to being a Regional Manager over a thousand people. Kyle and his family moved several times. The child found himself confused and even depressed at times. Standing out in a crowd was no longer a given, and friendships came, but with much effort. The new friendships were seemingly empty in comparison to earlier friendships. The next four years became a peculiar time. Kyle's long standing friendships from the early days were in the past. Kyle was no longer "Mr. Popularity" or "The King of Smiles." For the first time in his life, he was just an ordinary boy, and that knowledge made him sad.

By the end of sixth grade, Kyle began experiencing severe headaches that grew progressively worse all summer. It was the darkest time of his life. The pain incapacitated him, and his eyes were so sensitive to light that he could not stand a ray of sunlight in his room. After spending a couple of months in painful seclusion, doctors at long last accurately diagnosed him as having a condition known as Hydrocephalus, also known as "water on the brain." It was a life-threatening condition without surgical intervention.

The human body manufactures and accumulates Cerebral Spinal Fluid (CSF) that drains naturally, being absorbed within the body. In Hydrocephalus patients, the CSF is not absorbed as expected and it collects within the ventricles of the head, causing abnormal pressure on the brain, and in turn causing severe and unrelenting headaches. This condition is fairly common in very young children, 1 in 500, but considered uncommon in children in their teen years. Hydrocephalus emerging unprompted in older children without injury or following a disease like Meningitis happens to only 1 in a million.

Kyle was 12 years old when he entered the hospital for the first brain surgery. He was frightened and confused. His family did not attend church or acknowledge God in their lives, so Kyle did not understand to whom he might turn for hope and peace of mind. All he could do was trust his Neurosurgeon, hoping for the best as they attempted to implant a brain shunt. The surgery went well.

A brain shunt is a narrow piece of tubing that is inserted into the brain in the fluid-filled ventricle. The tubing is then passed under the skin into another area of the body, most often into the stomach. Occasionally, the shunt tubing may be placed into one of the chambers of the heart or the lining of the lungs. The shunt tubing releases pressure on the brain, by depleting the extra fluid in the brain ventricles and re-routing it to a different area of the body where it can be absorbed more quickly.

Over the next few years, Kyle's shunt malfunctioned 15 times, requiring surgical intervention each time. The once happy child changed into one who was quiet, reserved, and struggling to find a glimpse of the smile that once defined him.

In preparation for the sixth surgery, Kyle found himself lying on a gurney in "Pre-Op," awaiting his turn to enter the Operating Room. There in the stillness, he realized he was becoming sad and discouraged, but mostly from concern for his parents. He disliked causing them grief and worry, especially his mom. She was his main care-giver, and with each surgery she worried herself sick. Kyle's sickness and surgeries had taken a noticeable toll on her.

All of a sudden, a thought entered Kyle's mind! Pray, just pray! he thought to himself. "I don't really know God, but what better time to get to know Him!" There in the silence, Kyle prayed his very first prayer. He said to God, "If You really exist, please know that I don't like seeing my parents suffer while watching me go through all of this, so can You just let me die during surgery so they can move on with their lives?"

Moments later, the Holy Spirit rested on young Kyle and the

peace of God settled into his being. It was unlike anything he had experienced before. He was convinced that God heard him and would answer by letting him die during the procedure.

> *Peace I leave with you, My peace I give unto you: not as the world giveth, give I unto you. Let not your heart be troubled, neither let it be afraid* (John 14:27 KJV).

As Kyle regained consciousness in the Recovery Room, a nurse told him his pulse had dropped significantly right after surgery; they almost lost him. She thought they might have to resuscitate him, yet strangely, his vital signs returned to normal without medical intervention! She assured him that all was well and that he was going to be just fine!

At that moment, Kyle heard the loving and gentle voice of the Holy Spirit speaking to his own spirit saying, "I am not ready to take you yet; there is something you must do first." A wonderful feeling came over him! That holy whisper breathed much needed life and hope into the heart of one who was floundering and in need of strong Heavenly encouragement! It was the time when God's sweet divine intervention changed Kyle's perspective; for the very first time he experienced hope!

Incredibly, Kyle still had 9 brain surgeries and a mini stroke ahead of him due to shunt malfunctions. All those surgeries came in the next 2 years. During that time, a ruptured appendix presented its own set of complications, putting him in a near-death situation in the hospital for four weeks. Suffering had woven itself into the fabric of Kyle Bates' life. Patience was born as a result of endurance and perseverance working in unison with the suffering.

Consider it all joy my brethren, when you encounter various trials, knowing that the testing of your faith produces endurance. Let endurance have its perfect result, so that you may be perfect and complete, lacking in nothing (James 1:2-4).

There were many questions looming, and so few answers in Kyle's mind. Psychologically and spiritually, this young man needed more clarity. Once again, he was in dire need of holy consolation. He questioned why his life had changed from good to bad, why he had come close to death so many times, yet lived. He wanted a direction to go in and a goal to strive for, but first things first. God wanted to be first in Kyle's life!

The Lord sent Kyle three new friends who knew Jesus as their personal Savior. Each one of them had a personal relationship with Jesus. That seemed foreign to Kyle, yet appealing and inviting at the same time. Could this relationship be the one he was searching for all along? Could Jesus somehow fill the void left by lost friendships and changing times? Kyle began reading his Bible and actively seeking the Lord in the years that followed.

At the age of 19, after seeking God and searching for answers in His Word, Kyle ended up at a church service in Houston, Texas. In a voice that was only a whisper, Kyle prayed, "Lord, I want to give You my life today, but I am scared. There are so many people here, they will see me and look at me. Help me please!" Although he was afraid at first, Kyle decided to surrender his life to God at that very moment! Two strong, invisible hands lovingly lifted Kyle from his seat, gently escorting him forward. If his feet touched the floor, he was unaware of it! He was weeping and extremely conscious of the loving presence of God in him and all around him!

A supernatural transformation took place, washing away the "old self" and making him brand new! Forgiveness came when Jesus entered his heart, granting him Salvation. He acknowledged that Jesus Christ bore his sins, suffered and died on the cross, having paid the price for his Salvation. A change of heart and a changed mind came to live in Kyle. That day he became a born again believer, a child of the Most High God. It was an extraordinary experience, a miracle undeniably!

Kyle lived for 22 years without having another surgery. His faith and love for God increased. God's love for him became more evident each day. Kyle began searching for the woman with whom he was to spend his life. His first serious romance failed. After the dissolution of that unsuccessful relationship, the Lord mysteriously led Kyle to the woman he was destined to marry! During a time of soul-searching, Kyle ended up with a co-worker named Desiree. He needed a good listener, who would understand what he was going through. Desiree and Kyle were friends, having worked together for two years. Their first real conversation lasted all night, and strangely, by the next morning, each one knew they would spend their lives together. They started making wedding plans on their second date!

Falling in love did not happen overnight. It was godly wisdom that led them to pray for God's guidance. They prayed together, asking God to "send them love to match the vision they each had in their hearts, to be husband and wife." The Lord provided, giving each one a deep and sincere love for the other that would be life changing!

Four months later, Kyle and Desiree were married! While on their honeymoon in Maui, Hawaii, they prayed God would send them their first child in five more years. Five years later, God sent them an adorable baby girl! Two more children would follow!

God began blessing Kyle. Over the next 20 years, he worked in a business where success was measured by the accomplishment of sales. In due time, he became a Corporate Sales Coach over a team of 150 representatives. With God's guidance and help, he helped his team improve sales above and beyond all expectations. Kyle became increasingly successful in his career and once again Kyle became aware of a strange, yet familiar force operating in his spirit. Pride reared its ugly head as it did when he was a young boy.

In 2010 Kyle suffered an Intracranial Bleed. It nearly cost him his life, leaving him in an altered state of mind for the next six months. Eight hour time periods vanished with Kyle not realizing they had occurred. At times he could hear words, although he could not respond. Extended memory lapses were common in those days. Kyle's wife, his gift from God, prayed faithfully for Kyle, believing he would be healed. God restored much of his health.

Throughout the years God saved Kyle from death's grip many times. Following the 2010 surgery, God caused Kyle to understand there would never be a place in his life where pride would be tolerated.

Kyle's own words revealed much when he said, "I now have a thorn in my side, so to speak, as a reminder to me of all that pride has wrought". Looking back on it all, Kyle has a new comprehension. In his present day spiritual maturity, he is able to see that even at a young age, pride had entered his life. It is essential for everyone to understand the full implications of that dreaded sin. Pride is one of the seven deadly sins. Pride is the root of all sin. It causes us to turn away from God. Notice that both words "pride" and "sin" have the letter "I" in the middle! All disobedience and rebellion have pride as its root.

Pride goes before destruction, and a haughty spirit before a fall (Proverbs 16:18).

Kyle's journey that began with the suffering, allowed him to encounter many experiences. However, it is what Kyle avoided that makes his story worth telling and re-telling! Pride might have destroyed his life, but suffering kept him from that fate! Kyle's message to humanity is this: "Pride is the most serious and subtle of all sins and must be avoided at all costs! In order to avoid it, you must acknowledge that it exists! People of all ages are susceptible to pride and its sinful consequences!"

There is a contrast between the kind of pride that God hates and the kind of pride we take in doing a good job at work. The kind of pride that stems from self-righteousness is sin, and God loathes it because it is a deterrent to seeking Him. The proud are so consumed with themselves that their thoughts are far from God. This kind of haughty pride is contrary to the spirit of humility that God teaches us that we must have if we are to be pleasing to Him.

The wicked in the haughtiness of his countenance does not seek God and his thoughts are, "There is no God" (Psalm 10:4).

Blessed are the poor in spirit: for theirs is the Kingdom of Heaven (Matthew 5:3).

The "poor in spirit" are those who recognize their absolute spiritual impoverishment and their inability to come to God aside from His grace. The proud are so blinded by their pride that they think they have no need of God. They believe God should be honored to receive them as they are, since they are convinced that they deserve His acceptance.

Kyle wants readers to understand that his suffering became his friend. With the passage of time, he became very thankful for the ways in which the suffering affected him! Suffering put an end to his pride and taught him the meaning of humility. At the young age of 12, Kyle was nearing the time where he would be confronted with decisions, having to choose his path in life; one path leading to the left and one path leading to the right. One path would lead to Heaven and the other would lead to hell! Kyle's journey afforded him the opportunity to encounter many priceless benefits of personal surrender to the Most High God. These Godly benefits are available for all who surrender in humility to God, while the dispensation of "Grace" is still available. Where there is life there is hope!

"For I know the plans I have for you," declares the LORD, "plans to prosper you and not to harm you, plans to give you HOPE and a future" (Jeremiah 29:11 NIV).

Chapter 40

Kindred Spirits

Look at the birds of the air, that they do not sow, nor reap nor gather into barns, and yet your Heavenly Father feeds them. Are you not worth much more than they? (Matthew 6:26).

During the years of Bob Munson's retirement life, he was a commercial fisherman on the Delaware Bay. Time spent on the water was a pleasurable experience for Bob! When Bob brought in his "catch," often times there were some fish that he would save for his wife, Jean to prepare for their dinner. The bulk of the "catch" was routinely bait fish he caught for local crabbers. Whenever he cleaned the food-fish, Bob saved the scraps for the seagulls. The seagulls regularly gathered overhead waiting for Bob to toss their providential morsels high into the air! Bob saw the seagulls as kindred spirits!

Bob and Jean were living in Newport, New Jersey when Bob's doctor discovered he was suffering from esophageal cancer. The terrible news was devastating! The loving couple of 60 years made the very best of the time they had left. Jean fortified her faith by praying and reading books about true miraculous occurrences and she learned how God often speaks to His children in times of grief. Jean was comforted and a little surprised by some of the ways in which the Lord had evidenced Himself to people in some of the stories using various means including clouds, birds and even roses!

On the day of Bob's death, Jean and their son and daughter came together with Bob in his room. They treasured the remaining hours and minutes that lessened like sand pouring through the narrow throat of a sand clock or an hour glass. It was a peaceful time for a well lived life rapidly coming to a close. The Hospice Chaplin had prayed with Bob earlier in the day and he was very much at peace with his imminent transition. Bob died at home with his family by his bedside and they were aware that he left them on "wings of prayer"!

After Bob's funeral the adult children returned to their out-of-state homes, leaving their mom alone for the very first time. Jean was naturally sad, and her tears flowed freely as she reconciled within her heart what the future held for her as a widow. Seeking solace, Jean re-read portions of her books about miraculous occurrences, hoping God would show up in her hours of need.

It was late in the afternoon when Jean walked to her small garden behind the barn, searching for some red ripe tomatoes. It was late September, and fresh tomatoes on the vines would not last much longer. Jean felt utterly abandoned as she walked slowly toward the garden. She looked up into a perfectly beautiful cloudless blue sky! Flying in just then, she noticed a flock of seagulls soaring in from the Bay direction. As she picked tomatoes, Jean became aware that the seagulls were "keeping vigil" it seemed, staying constantly present above her!

Jean thought to herself, "We never have seagulls this far inland when the skies are clear and blue!" Suddenly, she was overwhelmed by a sense of Bob's presence, his loving spirit and the assurance of his tender and ever present love. It flooded her soul! Jean sensed Bob's presence was somehow connected to the visiting seagulls! The gulls did not leave Jean even while she walked homeward that day. When she reached the house she sat on the porch, watching and enjoying the show the seagulls were putting on seemingly for her benefit! They continued flying and wheeling overhead, leaving only when Jean went inside!

Standing just inside the house and looking through the window panes, Jean was amazed by the out- pouring of God's love and Bob's love she had just experienced! And to think, it was demonstrated by a flock of seagulls! She stood there watching as the birds left the area, flying back in the direction of the Bay, 6 miles away!

For your Maker is your husband--the LORD Almighty is His name (Isaiah 54:5 NIV).

The experience affected Jean in a powerful way, affirming to her that "all was well with Bob's soul"! She knew deep in her heart that she would be able to rejoice in the confirmation of faith shared by both of them! God had generously provided evidence of His holy presence in a time when He was greatly needed. That precious knowledge would be a great consolation to Jean in the days ahead!

But they that wait upon the LORD shall renew their strength; they shall mount up with wings as eagles; they shall run, and not be weary; and they shall walk, and not faint (Isaiah 40:31 KJV).

Chapter 41

An Angel was There

For He Himself has said, "I will never desert you, nor will I ever forsake you" (Hebrews 13:5).

The pronouncement, "You have lung cancer," produces a sobering and chilling effect, impacting the lives of the patient and those who love that person. Seth Albright was quick to say he could accept those words in regard to himself more easily than he could have accepted them pertaining to his wife, Karen.[15] Seth was a strong guy, as tough as nails, and if one of them had to die, he was glad it was him. His heart was in the right place, wanting to spare his wife from physical pain. Karen promised herself she would not let him know that her emotional pain cut deeper than his physical pain. Seth's pain would soon end. Karen's pain was only beginning.

The oncologist insisted on getting a Positron Emission Tomography (PET) scan. That is a technique most commonly used for imaging metabolic activity in the human body and it determines which areas of the body have been affected by the disease, in addition to the previously known location. They both agreed to the study even though it could last up to 75 minutes.

Lying flat was impossible for Seth, due to the large amounts of fluid that accumulated recurrently in his chest even after having a Thoracentesis procedure performed. That procedure was accomplished when a doctor inserted a long needle directly into the chest cavity, the area surrounding the lungs, by drawing off as much

---

15

excess fluid as he could. The relief from the procedure was brief and temporary. The pain and inability to breathe returned consistently, with even greater intensity than before.

There was some small apprehension the morning of the PET scan because Seth could not lie flat. When he tried to lie flat, it decreased his breathing ability significantly. He could not lift his arm under his own strength for more than a minute or two. He would have to do both if the test was to be completed. The attending nurse advised Karen she would have to leave Seth because no one was allowed in the testing area while a scan was in progress. With much kind persuasion, Karen appealed to the nurse for understanding because she really wanted to be with Seth. Increasingly, he appeared to need her beside him more and more with each passing hour. The cancer had progressed to the point where Seth felt like he was drowning much of the time and it was a frightening experience.

The nurse finally consented and Karen went to Seth's side. His eyes lit up and a slow smile crossed his face at the sight of her! Karen propped a pillow under one side of Seth, giving him a little relief from the uncomfortable position he was in. She was able to lift his arm fully, supporting it with her strength so he could just let go for several minutes at a time. They took turns supporting the full weight of his left arm and shoulder. When his mouth became too dry, Karen poured water from her water bottle into the bottle cap, then poured tiny sips inside his lower lip. Each time, Seth nodded and smiled in silence.

It was an unpleasant hour and a half and there in the silence, their thoughts were exchanged without a single spoken word. Suddenly Karen became aware of someone else in the room with them! She looked toward the right side of the room from where she was standing. There it was! She saw a soft glowing white light about four feet tall in the shape of an egg! The light was not the least bit intimidating, although it was not a human being. The shimmering white light pulsed, ever so gently, as if it was breathing. It did not have a face, but it radiated energy of love, peace, calmness, and the definite assurance that it was a holy presence. The angel being did not speak. It simply made its presence known reminding Karen and Seth they were not alone.

Karen looked down at Seth, telling him, "There's an angel in the room with us. Can you see it?"

Seth nodded once. He then added, "The angel is standing over towards your right side."

Seth and Karen received a great deal of strength and comfort from knowing God was watching what they were going through. Each one comprehended that no matter what happened in the coming days, they would get through it all by God's grace and His provision.

Seth died one week after the angel appearance. Was there sadness, grief, and pain from his death and departure? To be sure it was, but it was all bearable. The whole life changing cancer ordeal was viewed from a different perspective after God graciously and generously made His presence positively known to the family. The presence reminded them that death does not cause the deceased to cease to exist. Death is merely the vehicle that carries the very much alive spirit into an after-life of eternal Heaven or eternal Hell.

Seth had made the sincere decision to receive Jesus as his Savior as a young man, therefore his place in Heaven was reserved and certain. The Apostle Paul's words recorded in the Bible offers much hope to those who are saved!

For we walk by faith, not by sight-- we are of good courage, I say, and prefer rather to be absent from the body and to be at home with the Lord. Therefore we also have as our ambition, whether at home or absent, to be pleasing to Him (2 Corinthians 5:7-9).

Chapter 42

The Crash

The LORD will keep you from all evil; He will keep your life. The LORD will keep your going out and your coming in from this time forth and forevermore (Psalm 121:7-8).

Cindy Benning[16] climbed out of bed, already longing for her first cup of coffee! She made her way to the kitchen while yawning. Ten minutes later, Cindy was comfortably reclining in her favorite chair, sipping coffee and reading her Bible. It was what she did every day as regularly as clockwork. Prayer time would follow, then a thirty minute exercise routine. When she failed to hold fast to that routine of placing God first, her days had been known to simply fall apart. With age comes wisdom, and Cindy had discovered the spiritually rich consequences of making God first in every facet of her life; not just a haphazard careless attempt either.

"What do I do today?" was Cindy's question as she contemplated her daily responsibilities and prioritized mentally. She flipped the switch on a small lamp on the sofa table, but nothing happened. "Just a blown bulb," she considered, while walking toward the garage where she kept a large box of various sizes of bulbs. She located a 40 watt bulb and replaced the bad bulb, but once again nothing happened. What to do now? She really did like that lamp a lot and the lamp stayed on most of the time; she knew she would have to replace it. No more asking what to do first! Going to a home

---

16

improvement store or a department store to buy a new lamp suddenly topped her "to do" list!

The second stop allowed Cindy to find a suitable replacement lamp, which she purchased before heading home. She found herself driving through a large shopping center parking lot. As she drove, a soft, calm voice spoke to her in the aloneness of her automobile saying, "Pray for safety!"

At once Cindy responded by praying a quick one-liner, "Father keep me safe; I plead the blood of Jesus over me and this car." About five seconds later she stopped at a 4-way stop sign, looking both ways and seeing that all was clear. The traffic lanes to her left and to her right were divided lanes, separated by tall landscaping shrubs. A stop would definitely be required by all drivers approaching the 4-way stop because of the limited sight created by the shrubbery. Feeling safe, she accelerated while moving forward.

As soon as she was in the middle of the drive-through space, she saw something in her right-sided peripheral vision. It was a fast moving white SUV, and the driver was not stopping at the sign! Cindy hit her brakes instinctively, while realizing it was too late; a collision was already in progress!

At that moment the SUV impacted her small car on the passenger side near the front tire and front passenger door. She could see the frightened face of the woman driving the SUV and her facial expression was one of sheer terror! It was the strangest thing Cindy had ever experienced!

On five previous occasions, in a 35 year period, her car had been hit by other vehicles driven by drivers who failed to yield. Each of those incidents happened because drivers had carelessly or accidentally driven into her car. Each time, there was a dreaded sound of crushing metal against metal, crumpling under pressure from the powerful impact. Cindy had never been injured seriously. However, there was always that sense of dread and the unavoidable sounds of the cars crashing!

But not that time; instead there was an eerie sound of silence as if all the ordinary sounds of the world had been sucked out by a vacuum. There was only a peculiar stillness surrounding the scene at the intersection. Cindy saw the SUV hit her car with so much force that each car should have been significantly damaged. After a few moments of wide-eyed alarm demonstrated by both drivers, the offending driver reversed her SUV, backed out of the collision, seemingly unaffected by the crash, and then sped away as fast as she could go! Cindy drove out of harm's way before stopping and inspecting her car. There was no damage to Cindy's car. She climbed back in her car and sat there for the longest time, trying to make sense of what had just happened.

Being an avid reader, Cindy had read of instances where drivers claimed they had experienced similar episodes. She recalled a woman who claimed an out-of-control tractor trailer "big-rig" drove through her van on an icy road. That frantic woman and her hysterical passenger both watched it happen as they screamed in horror! Another motorist driving toward them saw the incident and confirmed the mysterious occurrence. Two vehicles actually drove through each other as if they were made of air. There were no injuries and no damage to either of the vehicles could be found. There was no explanation for that incident and Cindy could not explain what just happened to her. Divine intervention, God's holy protection was the only possible explanation!

Later, Cindy drove toward her neighborhood with her new lamp, feeling tremendously blessed, knowing God had warned her to pray immediately before the crash, knowing God had protected those involved in the super-natural car crash!

Arriving back at her home, Cindy plugged in the new lamp and flipped the switch. Nothing happened. At first she was disturbed, then she carried the lamp to another electrical outlet to determine if her problem was two defective lamps or a bad outlet. The new lamp still did not work, so she put it aside until she could make time to return it for a refund. She put the old defective lamp back in its original place because it filled the empty space, and out of habit she flipped the switch. What do you know! The light came on as if there had never been a problem!

Cindy sat for a few moments, thinking of the series of events and her unnecessary trip to replace a lamp that was not defective at all. If the lamp had not failed, she would not have gone to the shopping area, the place of her "near miss." There would have been no need for the Lord to speak to her, warning of impending danger. The car crash and super-natural delivery would never have taken place.

Could it all have been a test of faith and an obedience lesson, perhaps a trial run for some later occurrence at which time she would act quickly because of her lesson that day? That was a possibility! It was the only reasonable explanation, so Cindy accepted it, thanking God for everything that happened. She contented herself, knowing that one day she would understand more about the ways of God, in His perfect timing.

My times are in Your hand (Psalm 31:15).

Chapter 43

Take My Hand

Fear not, for I am with you; be not dismayed, for I am your God; I will strengthen you, I will help you, and I will uphold you with My righteous right hand (Isaiah 41:10).

The day was May 17, 1971 and Edward Clark was only 17 years old. He and his family were living in Elk City, Oklahoma at the time. Just before eleven o'clock that Saturday morning, Edward decided he needed a haircut and that is why he headed to town. It was an average day, just like any other day as far as young Edward was concerned.

Although he was only 17, Edward had given some serious thought to the subject of dying because it was the Vietnam War era, and his 18th birthday was fast approaching. At that time he would be drafted if he did not voluntarily enter into some branch of military service. That is why he gave dying a second thought. He wondered if on the last day of his life, he would wake up early that particular morning, feeling any different than he felt on any other day. It was a morbid thought, but war-time was a serious time, especially if you were a young man thinking of joining the army or of being drafted. Edward didn't dwell on those thoughts, but certainly he had wondered what it would be like to die. In reference to death, he thought of dying as a soldier; but never in his wildest dreams did he think of dying that very day!

Edward climbed onto his 1970 Honda CB-350 motorcycle, started the engine with a loud roar and made his way toward the barber shop. By noon, he was heading home, traveling through a residential area. He was south-bound and approaching an intersection where he had the right of way. In his peripheral vision Edward caught a glimpse of a light blue sedan heading west, traveling approximately 45 miles per hour, and immediately, he knew the driver had no intention of stopping at the stop sign. He was right.

It all happened so fast! Edward knew he could not stop in time and even if he locked his brakes, the best he could do was collide with the fast moving car! He thought his best chance for survival was to open up the throttle and literally fly across the intersection before the car reached him. It was a good plan, but it didn't work out the way he hoped it would. The sedan impacted Edward's motorcycle on the left rear side, knocking the bike out from under him! The impact hurled Edward into the air! He saw his left shoe strangely tumbling slowly in the air two feet above his head just before his body hit the concrete.

Edward slid thirty feet along the pavement until his body slammed into a cement curb; he then bounced away from it. He never knew a human body could bounce but in fact, it can; and it did! He could hear the metallic crushing sound of the bike grinding its way along on the pavement, coming to a complete stop a few feet from where he landed.

A searing pain hit Edward instantly, and he clearly understood that he was seriously injured. The pain seemed to be throughout his whole body so he couldn't tell how many bones were broken or how badly he was scraped and cut. The sharp pain that took his breath away was coming from his back, the spinal area. Very soon, an ambulance arrived, and the EMT's slid a body board beneath his pain-ridden body. They pulled him securely into a safe position on the board before lifting him onto the stretcher. That was the last thing Edward remembered from the scene of the accident. Mercifully, his world turned black, sounds decreased into silence and he lost consciousness.

The ambulance transported the injured man toward the nearest emergency room. Meanwhile, Edward died. He left his body and embarked upon a journey that took him out of his body. At first, everything was solid black and he saw nothing. Slowly, there appeared a very large light in the darkness; the intensity increased until it was nearly blinding! It grew into an enormous brilliant white light! Edward knew that where ever he was, it surely was a peaceful place; he felt very calm and very tranquil. Next, he saw his mom and dad, both of whom were still living and well, standing to the left side of the white light, holding hands! They were extending their free hands towards him saying, "Son, please come back to us!"

At that moment, Edward's attention moved to the space just above him and he saw a very large right hand reaching down for him. Suddenly, he heard a powerful voice speaking to him saying, "Ed, take my hand!" He was very frightened and used both his hands to push the outstretched hand away from his body! That physical and emotional move propelled him away from the extended hand and back into consciousness where he regained consciousness in the emergency room! He was in the most excruciating pain imaginable!

As Edward came back into consciousness in the emergency room, he realized he could see but all of his other senses were oddly absent. He could visually see nurses working on him but he could not hear any sounds. There was only silence. He could feel the touches of the nurses but he could not move. His brain attempted to send messages to his limbs to make them move, but his tries were unsuccessful.

Suddenly Edward was aware of a sensation like an electrical current entering the top of his head then slowly traveling downward through his entire body. The electricity traveled down his spine and into each arm, and through his back, then downward to his legs. It was at that time that he felt life being restored to his body. With the restoration of his senses came an agonizing pain that increased seemingly with each minute! The nurses began administering strong pain killers, one of which was Demerol, to decrease the tormenting pain.

He had returned to life! Edward's decisions to reject the outstretched hand and to stay on earth would take him into a time of suffering unlike anything he had ever known. He suffered multiple fractures of the lumbar vertebrae that resulted in paralysis from his waist down. He was scraped and bruised in various places; none of those injuries were life-threatening. He faced many months of recuperation and rehabilitation if he ever hoped to walk again.

A time of wearisome medical treatment, distressing physical therapy, and hard work lay ahead of Edward. In addition to the suffering, he would have to learn to walk all over again. Edward discovered he was actually very fortunate because his paralysis was not permanent. After many months of working toward his goal of walking, Edward did just that. It was a difficult recovery, but slowly, he did regain his ability to walk.

Four months after the accident, Edward received his Draft Notice in the mail, instructing him to report for Active Duty. His Selective Service number was #32. Even though he did recuperate from the accident, he was physically impaired to the point that he was never physically able to enter the Armed Forces. He often wondered if the accident that kept him from serving in Vietnam actually saved his life. He would never know the answer for sure.

Many years have come and gone since the accident, and to this day, Edward still questions his reasons for rejecting the hand of God that was ready and willing to take him out of this life that unforgettable day. Now that he is more than 60 years old, he knows this one thing for certain. He remarked, "The next time I find myself in a restful peaceful place like the place I entered when I died back then, I know this much. I will not be afraid to take the right hand of my Lord and Savior when He comes for me! Next time, I will be ready to go with Him!"

Come to Me (Jesus Christ), all who are weary and heavy-laden, and I will give you rest (Matthew 11:28).

Chapter 44

A Test of Faith

If you abide in Me, and My Words abide in you, ask whatever you wish, and it will be done for you (John 15:7).

When Dianne Pace's youngest son was a toddler, she noticed his chest was becoming depressed. As time passed and the child grew, the depression became more noticeable. When the concerned mother took him for his regular visit to the Pediatrician, she inquired about the abnormality. The doctor was not concerned and said it was called a "depressed sternum". He even said his own younger brother had the same condition and it had not impacted his life adversely. The physician said the only thing she needed to watch for or be concerned about was shortness of breath. If the boy developed that condition, that would be evidence of a serious problem.

Time passed quickly, and the toddler grew strong and reached his pre-teen years, at which time the depressed sternum appeared to be extremely depressed. Dianne noticed her son having bouts with "shortness of breath," although the boy denied it. Perhaps it was subtle, and he was not even aware of the condition. Dianne made arrangements for her son to see a well-respected Thoracic Surgeon at a Children's Hospital in Birmingham, Alabama. Diagnostic studies were performed, and the results indicated a serious condition was indeed present.

The boy's heart had shifted from the left center of his chest to the extreme left side of his chest because of the depression. Surgery was needed to correct the abnormality and if surgical intervention was not carried out at once, there would come a time when the heart would be damaged irreversibly. The surgeon clearly warned the family about the operation, saying it would be an intense surgery, carried out over a long period of time, perhaps 12 hours. He warned them to get prepared for what was ahead.

Because the family was a Christian family, they had always faced their trials with an attitude of faith; praying and trusting God for His divine intervention and healing power. This time would be no different. On the day of the surgery, several family members, their church pastor, and some of their close friends drove 100 miles to be with their family while the surgery was under way. They offered many prayers before the procedure and the day of the surgery.

The morning passed fairly quickly, but the afternoon minutes and hours ticked slowly by. When darkness came, Dianne encouraged some of their entourage to go home, saying all was well and in God's hands. It took almost 13 hours for the surgeon to finish the operation. The boy ended up in the Intensive Care Unit initially; however, after many days had passed, the doctor released him to go home under the watchful eyes of his parents.

When they arrived home that day, Dianne was physically and emotionally drained, having very little strength left. There was no time to "let her guard down" because she had to go to the grocery store to buy special foods for the post-surgery patient. It was Sunday, so the store might not be crowded. Dianne rushed to get there, and grabbed a grocery cart and dashed down the first aisle. She was in need of canned soups, "Jell-O," juices and anything else that her boy might want to eat and might digest easily.

Dianne started down the first aisle and she noticed a lady standing at the canned soup section. She was wearing a scarf, partially covering her head and face. As Dianne passed the woman, she spoke saying, "Hello Dianne, how are you doing?" Dianne responded by saying she was just fine and continued shopping.

As she started down the next aisle, she saw the same woman standing at the "Jell-O" section, the same place she was headed for. As Dianne arrived at the "Jell-O" section, the woman turned and looked into her face, and she said, "Hello Dianne." Dianne said "hello" again, and she was puzzled. The woman was very kind and spoke with the calmest voice. Her eyes were beautiful and her expression was one of compassion and kindness. Dianne had never seen the woman before and wondered who she was and how she knew her name. She was too tired to worry about it.

Dianne neared the end of the aisle and ran into a friend who commented about the woman wearing the scarf. The stranger had spoken to the friend, calling her by name as well. Both women were confused. Still, the stranger inspired a sense of calmness and caring consideration to Dianne as if she knew everything she and her family had been going through.

When Dianne headed for the checkout counter, she was overcome by curiosity and felt compelled to go back and talk to that woman. She moved quickly from one side of the store to the other looking down the nearly empty Sunday morning store aisles. The stranger was nowhere to be found!

Dianne paid for her groceries and loaded the bags into her car then began her drive home. Suddenly, from the back seat of her car, Dianne heard a soothing voice speaking to her saying, "And you shall entertain angels unaware."

Tears began to flow down her face, seemingly washing away the overwhelming stress and pressure she had been under for such a long time during the hospitalization. She thought she needed to pull over because her entire body began to shake as with a holy manifestation! The presence of God overwhelmed her! It all became so clear to her then, that God was with her and had been with her boy through it all, providing His wonderful care and provision that only He had power to give! God had sent an angel to remind her He cared and that He had many helpers to help her along the way! She experienced a well-needed sense of relief!

Dianne never saw the lady after that day, but says she thinks of her often, and each time she remembers her lovely eyes! She hopes to see her again one day when Jesus calls her home to Heaven; perhaps the stranger will lead her to the Gates of Heaven. Dianne hopes that will happen, because she wants to tell her, "Thank you!"

Always giving thanks to God the Father for everything, in the name of our Lord Jesus Christ (Ephesians 5:20 NIV).

Chapter 45

Her Gift was Hope

And now, Lord, for what do I wait? My Hope is in You (Psalm 39:7).

Alexandra Marshal[17] had a very normal happy life for many years before she entered a series of trials and tribulations. She was one of those people who could make you laugh on your worst day; her faith in God was what she based her life upon! Alex's light shone brightest on the darkest days because her spiritual gift was the gift of hope. She believed it was her God-given duty to lift the spirits of all who were sad and hurting for one reason or another.

Before reaching her fiftieth birthday, while living near Nashville, Tennessee, Alex lost her much loved husband. The two were inseparable, being best friends as well as husband and wife. Her loss was nearly unbearable, but realizing how every form of suffering is allowed or caused by God for the purpose of "growing" the sufferer, Alex accepted it. She shouldered her circumstances well, comprehending the certainty that her situation was unchangeable. Alex decided to use the tragedy as a "faith builder," enabling her to experience God on a new level. Little did she know her present trials were preparing her for even greater trials in the coming years!

Only four years after Alex became a widow, her health took a downward turn. During the next three years she spent much of her time in hospitals and in the offices of physicians who tried to alleviate her suffering and her symptoms. Alex's heart was referred

---

17

to as a "broken heart" and the doctors did their best to fix it. The first surgical treatment occurred when a surgeon attempted to implant a pace maker and a defibrillator inside Alex's' chest. She nearly died during the surgery, but she mysteriously revived and recovered. She had a close call with death!

Alex underwent two heart surgeries, one year apart, following the initial procedure. During the last surgery she suffered a stroke that ended her life. Alex was actually dead for 19 minutes in which the surgeon and nurses diligently fought to restore her to life. The medical team exhausted their efforts to restore a normal heart beat, but strangely, just as they decided to abort the resuscitation effort, Alex's heart fluttered softly at first, then grew stronger and stronger until her heart was beating normally again. The surgeon called the experience a true miracle, admitting he had given up when life miraculously returned to Alex's body!

Shortly after the Near-Death-Experience and the Out-of-Body-Experience, Alex was able to tell others what happened during those 19 minutes! Her spirit left her body when her heart stopped beating and she journeyed to an extraordinary land filled with incomprehensible white radiant lights! She could not say if the brilliant lights were angels or just part of God Himself! She called what she saw "The Light of God," saying it was just too glorious for words!

The deceased Alex visited with her deceased husband while she was in that shimmering land of amazing dazzling white light! She saw only his face, not his body, for a brief time; but it was long enough for him to give her a message! The man who was surely dead to those who remained on the earth told his deceased wife that she would have to go back to earth because it wasn't the appropriate time for her to die.

He instructed her to return to her body where she was to fight to live. He reminded her to keep her "light" shining, to go on encouraging others and offering hope to those who were hurting and hopeless! With a kind smile and gentle words, he thanked Alex for being a "light" in his life during their years together! He then disappeared from her sight, just moments before her spirit returned to her body in the Operating Room.

Alex made a fair recovery and lived an additional two years in which she was able to tell her story on numerous occasions, always giving God the glory for healing her and allowing her to see a preview of Heaven! When the time came for her final departure, Alex left her body swiftly and without warning leaving behind loved ones who knew full well she had arrived in Heaven "healthy and whole"! Her funeral was a celebration of life, as she would have wanted it to be! Her family could only imagine the joyous Heavenly welcome and family reunion that awaited Alex! They were greatly comforted by the knowledge that she had gone to live with the Lord for all time!

Surely goodness and mercy shall follow me all the days of my life: and I will dwell in the house of the LORD forever (Psalm 23:6 KJV).

Chapter 46

Angel Wings

He shall cover thee with His feathers, and under His wings shalt thou trust (Psalm 91:4 KJV).

It was one of the hottest days early August had to offer in 1993 to Cedarville, New Jersey. That Saturday afternoon, the coolest place Linda Hall could find for her baby boy, Milt, was the bathtub filled with just the right amount of room temperature water. She carefully placed the baby inside a bathtub ring, enabling him to sit upright in the tub while he splashed his little hands in the soothing bathwater!

The sweltering heat invaded every room of the house; Linda was wearing only a pair of shorts, a tank top and nothing on her feet, trying to stay cool and comfortable. During the baby's bath time, a very large horse fly entered the bathroom, making its presence known by the incessant buzzing noise it made as it circled the room repeatedly!

Linda picked up a hand towel, twisted it a little, forming it into a weapon of sorts, and then swung it at the horse fly, hoping to land a fatal blow! Linda and her husband Tom had just finished painting the bathroom the day before and they still had not replaced the light fixture cover. While striking out at the annoying insect, Linda powered a hard blow that landed on the exposed light bulbs near the ceiling.

There was a popping noise, the well lit room was suddenly darkened, and the floor was immediately covered with broken glass!

The baby chimed in saying, "Uh oh!" Linda stood still; momentarily very much aware that her feet were bare. She was surrounded by slivers of glass and greatly concerned about the baby in the tub there in the darkness.

She calmly said, "Dear God, please help me!" Next she told the baby to be very still and she walked to him, lifting him out of the tub, assuming that her feet were going to be cut to pieces! She did not feel any pain, neither did she hear any glass crunching as she walked across the floor. Linda carried the baby back across the glass covered floor and into the bedroom. She was pleased to see that there was not one scratch on him!

She proceeded to call one of her neighbors for help, and he was quick to offer assistance. When he arrived, Linda accompanied him to the bathroom door and when he walked across the floor, his shoes crushed some of the glass and the sound was very audible. He replaced the bulbs and he was able to see that the floor was literally covered with pieces of broken glass.

He left the bathroom, asking Linda how badly she was injured; how severely the glass had cut the bottoms of her feet. She was happy to tell him that the glass did not injure her feet at all. The neighbor expressed his curiosity as to how she could have escaped the glass that was all over the place! He commented, saying it was a miracle that she was not injured!

Through the years, Linda has shared that story more than once, and each time she expresses the only explanation that seems rational. She firmly believes that God sent her an angel the moment she called out to Him! She can only imagine that the angel spread forth its wings so that her feet never touched the floor…only angel's wings! This particular memory is well worth remembering for it is a reminder that indeed, angels are watching over us!

The cherubim (angels) had their wings spread upward, covering the mercy seat with their wings (Exodus 37:9).

Chapter 47

Holy "Canna-Lilies"

Consider the lilies, how they grow: they neither toil nor spin; but I tell you, not even Solomon in all his glory clothed himself like one of these (Luke 12:27).

It was early 1995; Meggie and Bill Leno[18] and their two children were finally living in their new home located in a small middle-Tennessee community. Meggie had worked tirelessly with the builder and the two of them successfully modified the house plans to fit their family. She was so happy over the way it all turned out that she could not stop smiling! An oversized kitchen, separate living spaces upstairs for the children and a large master suite downstairs adjacent to a screened in porch fit their needs perfectly!

They moved in before Thanksgiving and were able to enjoy the home along with their family and extended family members on Thanksgiving Day. Baked turkey and all the fixings filled the new home with such an inviting aroma! The enjoyable feast prepared and served that day marked the first of many heart-warming celebrations to come! The family knew they were exceedingly blessed! They were quick to say that all they had in this world, loved ones and belongings, was provided by the grace of God!

My grace is sufficient (2 Corinthians 12:9).

Late February came and a couple of warm days reminded Meggie it was time to plant the Canna-Lily bulbs along the chimney

18

wall. Since the plants would be tall and wobbly, she wanted them to rest partially against the eastern edge of the house. She located her small spade and the bag of bulbs she had purchased the week before. Joyfully, she made herself comfortable kneeling on the ground at her well-chosen planting place.

She contemplated the best spot to dig a hole, before forcefully breaking the ground with the sharp edge of the spade. As the blade cut through the dirt, Meggie's keen ears heard the cutting edge puncture something. It sounded like a knife slicing an apple. Carefully, she removed the spade, and working with her fingers she lifted a double-handful of loose soil.

Meggie could scarcely believe what she had just unearthed! It was a sprouting Canna-Lily bulb! The sprout was two inches long! It had not made its way through the top layer of dirt, so she had no way of knowing beforehand that it was there. Careful examination revealed a small cluster of healthy Canna-Lily bulbs, all green and sprouting in preparation for a springtime showing in a matter of days!

Surprise is hardly the word for what Meggie felt! A bull dozer, a back hoe, and dump trucks had worked for days on the site preparing for the home construction. Many loads of soil were trucked in to the site from a bordering property to make the site suitable for the creation of the house. There were no Canna-Lily bulbs there before construction began, so how in the world did the bulbs get there at the precise spot where she intended to plant them all along?

Meggie had no earthly explanation, but she did have a Heavenly explanation! She savored the moment, knowing that God had somehow caused those bulbs to be placed there when all the dirt was being pushed around. She planted the new bulbs alongside the existing bulbs then waited patiently for weeks, watching for the first sign of blooms!

Red Bud trees planted along the south fence near the kitchen side of the house had been her second wish. Meggie gave up on that idea because she was not able to locate any Red Bud trees for sale. She thought she would work on that project perhaps the next year.

The first weekend in June was when Bill began clearing some of the over-grown weeds and brush where they had intended to plant the Red Bud trees. By lunch time, Bill had cleared that area and it looked totally landscaped. He was wearing a broad smile when he entered the kitchen, insisting that Meggie accompany him out to the south fence. They walked together as he remained secretive until they were just feet from the fence. Bill knelt down on one knee, pointing to five tiny trees that were barely breaking ground along the fence line. Meggie was astounded to see five Red Bud trees bearing distinctive heart shaped leaves emerging from the dirt!

Who could have known they were there? Perhaps they were there as a result of some old roots lying deep in the ground there from days gone by. Maybe an angel swooped in, carrying a shovel, and planted them in the twilight! It did not matter how God placed them there! They were there and that was all that mattered! The two never questioned God's method of delivery! Bill and Meggie just laughed and shook their heads with eyes looking skyward while their lips naturally offered up words of thanksgiving and praise to the Lord above!

By July, the Canna-Lilies bloomed. The Holy angel-planted Cannas wore miniature green foliage, with blossoms flourishing in brilliant yellow with red center streaks! The store-bought Cannas grew to be tall stalks of greenery; all dressed up in beautiful pure red thriving blooms!

The Canna-Lily bulbs and the Red Bud trees were most unusual house-warming gifts from the true "Giver of gifts"! The Lord sees all and knows all and He absolutely loves giving us delightful gifts if we will only receive them with humble hearts, while giving glory to Him for what He has done!

Let them give glory to the LORD and declare His praise (Isaiah 42:12).

Chapter 48

Lights On

His lamp shone over my head, and by His light I walked through darkness (Job 29:3).

The time had passed so quickly. Marilyn Pepper[19] could hardly believe her husband had been dead for over five years. Her world was very different now that she was alone. A recent down-sizing move had left her with only one negative emotion about the process: a reluctance to leave fond memories behind. All of the memories she shared with her husband revolved around the old house and that particular neighborhood. However, the move was a necessary action and she would have to adapt!

There was still a lot of unpacking to do and the boxes at times seemed "bottomless"! Marilyn had lived in her new home a little over a month when she realized she had no idea in which box the night lights were stored. Surely they would "turn up" soon. The bathroom adjacent to her bedroom was in dire need of a night-light!

Small boxes lined one wall in the bathroom and closet area, making it cluttered and potentially dangerous if she walked there in the darkness of night. Marilyn made a mental note to buy night-lights the next time she went to the grocery store!

It was a Friday evening when sheer exhaustion set in, and Marilyn decided "enough was enough." She turned off the lights and fell into bed in a darkened room. She was asleep in only a few minutes. A short time later, something happened that startled Marilyn awake!

19

Her eyes popped open and she found herself lying in a well-lighted bedroom.

At first she was afraid to move; Marilyn remained motionless for a few moments, knowing she was alone in the house when she went to bed. Someone had obviously entered the house, because the bathroom light had positively been turned on!

Marilyn sat up, then placed her feet on the floor without making a sound. First, she entered the bathroom, then the closet. She found no sign of an intruder in either of those areas. Silently and methodically, the woman moved through the rest of the house looking for the person who turned on the light. After a thorough search, it became clear that no one had entered the house! All of the doors were locked and secure. She was baffled, but decided to turn the light switch off and go back to bed.

The night concluded uneventfully, and Marilyn got out of bed the next morning as if nothing had happened. It was an odd occurrence for which she had no explanation and she decided to ignore it. That day happened to be her birthday so she chose to take a break from setting up the house and unpacking.

Marilyn met her family for an early birthday dinner that evening, then returned home and got ready for bed. Remembering what happened the night before, she entered the bathroom and flipped each light switch on and off making sure the lights were all working fine. She climbed into bed in a darkened room and began taking some very deep breaths as she tried to relax, looking forward to a restful night.

After only a couple of minutes, something very peculiar happened! Simultaneously her ears heard the bathroom light switch snap and her eyes saw the light suddenly shining into the darkened room. Whatever or whomever it was toying with the lights wasted no time that night! The incident occurred before she ever drifted off to sleep!

Marilyn sprang up and dashed into the bathroom. The same recessed light above the tub was shining brightly! The stunned woman was very much aware of the fact that something other than a human being was in her bathroom! She stood there bathed in the light, becoming increasingly aware that she was not alone. Her eyes saw no presence; however, that did not lessen the presence she sensed! She knew her deceased husband was with her, proving his being there by flipping the light switch yet a second time!

Moments later, Marilyn returned to bed filled with awe and the certainty she had experienced a supernatural visit; it was undeniable! Why? Perhaps he was saying "Happy Birthday, I didn't forget!" Or maybe he was simply reminding her to install a night-light for her own safety. Perhaps her husband was allowing her to know his memory did not remain in the old house; that his memory traveled with her always!

These days Marilyn Pepper looks back on that incident, fondly believing her husband's visit was for the purpose of all of the above! What happened gave her great comfort and the assurance that she had done the right thing by moving into her new home! God sends us peace by mysterious ways!

The LORD lift up His countenance on you, and give you peace (Numbers 6:26).

Chapter 49

Angel Companions

Keep me as the apple of Your eye; Hide me in the shadow of Your wings (Psalm 17:8).

Carol Brown still enjoys gardening and plans to care for her flowers and tomato plants until the Lord takes her Home. She enjoys spending time outdoors in the warm Florida sunshine beneath a Heavenly canopy of blue sky! She has been known to work long hours, missing much needed rest periods. More than once, after a tiring day of gardening, Carol has lost her balance, nearly falling backwards, but each time, God has protected her!

She has had several close calls, but every single time before any harm can befall her; Carol has felt very strong invisible hands taking hold of her body under her arms, before setting her upright on her feet once more!

Isn't it marvelous knowing how God will supply us with "Angel Companions" when we advance toward our delicate years? That certain knowledge is far better than having any earthly Insurance Plan!

Chapter 50

A Book Called *Heaven Rules*

But He answered and said, "It is written, Man shall not live on bread alone but on every Word that proceeds out of the mouth of God" (Matthew 4:4).

Have you ever dreamed or thought of something memorable during the night-time only to awaken in the morning with little memory of the details? That has happened to me before. Paper and pen are on the night-stand when I go to bed at night. There have been times when I have scribbled notes in complete darkness.

One morning in early August of 2012, I awoke and glanced at a legal pad lying on the night-stand. The page was filled with words; however, I did not recall writing anything during the night! Inspection of the mysterious writing caused me to acknowledge that it was written by my hand. The words spoke to me in reference to a matter I had been considering for several weeks. The contemplated matter was actually about writing a book called *Heaven Rules*. The idea to write the book came to me as the result of reading the Bible in a compressed time-frame.

I had recently participated in reading the Bible, from cover to cover, in a compressed timeframe of less than 90 days. In reference to that action, by Divine Revelation, the Lord had imparted to me the name and the value of the process called ABC — Accelerated Bible Concept. My intention was to introduce the ABC and ABC Challenge in a book called *Heaven Rules*.

The ABC Challenge is a specific method by which anyone can tap into the power of the Bible in an unprecedented manner by accessing it in a specified timeframe. I understood that completion of the ABC Challenge required less than 90 days, and accessing the Word of God in that compressed time period produced astonishing results and life changes for me!

The end results were pronounced in contrast to the effects of reading the Bible at my leisure. The Lord provided insight regarding past reading experiences, revealing how reading the Word according to the Accelerated Bible Concept had actually affected others and me profoundly! The prior conclusions affected me spiritually, emotionally, and circumstantially. It became very obvious how that particular reading application triggered undeniable supernatural responses!

The mysterious night writing clearly indicated that I should proceed with *Heaven Rules*, in an expedient manner. These are the words that were written on the tablet and my understanding is that the Holy Spirit spoke those words, using my hand to write the message there in the darkness. The words were very readable and after reading the page several times, the message encouraged me greatly. Here are the words, and it seems like the Lord spoke to me first, then I made a reply before He continued to speak the remainder of His message. These are the words that were written on the paper:

"You give them something."

"But Lord, what do I have to give them?"

"Give them the pain that I have turned to joy. What I have revealed to you, what you have lived through and what you have experienced. It is only of value when you turn it into food for the hungry and balm for their pain. Give them your life experiences, the evidence of My presence. Give them the hope I have given to you. Show them how to survive the days of loneliness and tell them why those days come in the first place. Remember the sea of faces in "The Vision"? ("The Vision" referenced here is explained in detail in Chapter 17 of my first book of this series, *Real Messages from Heaven, Book 1*.) They cry out and I will send them hope through you, for you are My servant. My child, never underestimate My power!"

Almost immediately, the *Heaven Rules* project got underway! With each passing day, the Lord revealed more understanding about what He wanted me to share in the book. The concept was simple, yet very powerful. He wanted me to use the book as a teaching tool, sharing my testimony and many personal experiences that He had designed.

Heaven Rules was created to encourage people everywhere to embark on a remarkable spiritual journey, seeking a holy personal encounter with the living God, through His Holy Word! Reading the Bible deliberately takes us into the presence of God, and prolonged periods in close proximity to God changes us miraculously.

I completed *Heaven Rules* as soon as possible, making the book available to readers everywhere. No matter who we are or where we live, everyone needs a personal relationship with Jesus Christ! Many people are willing to seek Him, but they really do not know where to begin. *Heaven Rules* will help you find that starting place!

The Word, the Bible, is a powerful, supernatural instrument of communication with God. It is a means of tapping into the incredible love and power of our Heavenly Father. He desires to converse with us and to bless us in extraordinary ways! Accessing the Word according to ABC-Accelerated Bible Concept can cause real transformations!

Human beings live in a perpetual state of loneliness when they live separated from God. The loneliness only dissipates when we seek God's forgiveness for our sins, when we repent, surrendering our will, allowing Jesus to come into our hearts as Lord and Savior. The Bible reveals our hopelessness and creates an obvious desire in our hearts, to receive our Salvation!

A short time after *Heaven Rules* was released, many readers committed to taking The ABC Challenge. I heard from participants from all across the country. I was astounded by the response, and I clearly saw the need for *Heaven Rules*. I understood right away why the Lord made known to me the revelation that led to *Heaven Rules*. It was because so many people in the world were hurting and needing to discover His power in a unique way!

I have received amazing reports from numerous people who said they were reading the Bible for the first time in their lives and experiencing God in astonishing ways! Reading the Word according to ABC as presented in *Heaven Rules*, has produced amazing results! I have some knowledge of how ABC has affected many people. I have listed some of the results below.

- Prayers were miraculously answered during and after completion of the ABC Challenge.

- A marriage was restored after divorce.

- After the death of a loved one, the grieving process was made bearable by reading the Word as described in the ABC Challenge.

- An agnostic was converted to Christianity

- Several readers heard the Lord speak audibly to them.

- Some readers reported weight loss that came without effort. The only explanation being that the Word satisfied their inner cravings they had earlier tried to satisfy with food!

- One reported losing all desire for alcoholic beverages.

- Another reader was freed from a sexual addiction.

- One reader saw her blood pressure decrease from abnormally high to nearly normal.

- Many readers reported seeing sparkling particles of white light while reading the Word, believing that was evidence of the presence of the Holy Spirit.

I am convinced that ABC causes authentic and powerful life-changing transformations. I can only imagine what would happen if each person dedicated even one hour each day to reading the Word for the rest of their lives! The Word is so powerful that it can change our lives! It can easily change our hearts and minds, leading us to eternal Salvation! The Holy Word is available to each one of us who chooses to receive it as the divine gift that it truly is.

The ABC-Accelerated Bible Concept offers a remarkable advantage to people of all ages, who are searching for miraculous changes in their lives! I hope you will learn more about ABC by reading *Heaven Rules* in the near future! It is wise for each one of us to seek the Lord in His Word, while there is still time!

Prayer of Salvation

Dear God,
I confess that I have sinned in my lifetime and I am
sorry. I ask You to forgive me for my sins and I now
repent, and turn away from my sinful past. Jesus, I
ask You to come into my heart as my Lord and Savior.
Change my heart Lord, and make me be like You.

Thank You, Lord. In Jesus' name, I pray… Amen.

*If you confess with your mouth Jesus as Lord, and
believe in your heart that God raised Him from the
dead, you will be saved* (Romans 10:9).

Now, please ask that "The Holy Spirit" bear witness with your
spirit to confirm to you that you have been translated from the
kingdom of darkness to God's glorious Kingdom of Light through
the saving blood of Jesus Christ! Please be looking for this "witness"
immediately or in the days to come!

Remember to keep growing spiritually through daily reading of
God's Holy Word, The Holy Christian Bible! If you do not have a
good, readable version, please obtain one as soon as possible! An
excellent Bible choice is the one I have used for many years. It is the
"New American Standard Bible."

*For you have been born again, not of seed which is
perishable but imperishable, that is, through the Living
and Enduring WORD OF GOD* (1 Peter 1:23).

End Notes

1. The names in this chapter have been changed as requested.

2. The names in this chapter have been changed as requested.

3. The names in this chapter have been changed as requested.

4. The names in this chapter have been changed. pfa

5. The names in this chapter have been changed. pfa

6. The names in this chapter have been changed. pfa

7. The names in this chapter have been changed. pfa

8. The names in this chapter have been changed. pfa

9. Song composed by Binion, Brockman, Dufrene, Brown, and King. Integrity's Praise Music & Covenant Worship Group (adm. by EMI Christian Music Publishing); Soul Jive Music (adm. by Moon & Musky Music).

10. The names in this chapter have been changed. pfa

11. The names in this chapter have been changed as requested.

12. The names in this chapter have been changed. pfa

13. The names in this chapter have been changed. pfa

14. The names in this chapter have been changed. pfa

15. The names in this chapter have been changed. pfa

16. The names in this chapter have been changed. pfa

17. The names in this chapter have been changed as requested.

18. The names in this chapter have been changed. pfa

19. The names in this chapter have been changed. pfa

Note: The numbers shown above represent the end notes, not the chapter numbers.

Note: In reference to the end notes that end in the initials, pfa, please be advised that those stories are actually the author's experiences. She has chosen to change the names and tell the experiences in Third Person Omniscient.

When an author writes in third person omniscient, the readers are able to know and see many things about each character. Third person omniscient allows the author to have multiple voices in the story. By experiencing a story through different voices, we can see the story in another depth. We are also able to have a more objective interpretation of the events, meaning the interpretation is not influenced by personal feelings, as opposed to a more personal, subjective interpretation. Finally, an author may use third person omniscient because it allows for better storytelling and a more enjoyable reading experience for the reader!

Made in the USA
Middletown, DE
17 July 2015